COMPLETE CONDITIONING FOR BASKETBALL

National Basketball Conditioning Coaches Association

Bill Foran
Miami Heat

Robin Pound
Phoenix Suns 1991-2003

Editors

Human Kinetics

Library of Congress Cataloging-in-Publication Data

Complete conditioning for basketball / National Basketball Conditioning
Coaches Association ; Bill Foran, Robin Pound, editors.
    p. cm.
  Includes index.
  ISBN-13: 978-0-7360-5784-4 (soft cover)
  ISBN-10: 0-7360-5784-6 (soft cover)
  1. Basketball--Training. 2. Physical education and training. 3.
Physical fitness. I. Foran, Bill. II. Pound, Robin. III. National
Basketball Conditioning Coaches Association.
  GV885.35.C65 2007
  796.323--dc22
                          2007019292

  ISBN-10: 0-7360-5784-6
  ISBN-13: 978-0-7360-5784-4

Developmental Editor: Cynthia McEntire; **Assistant Editor:** Scott Hawkins; **Copyeditor:** Jan Feeney; **Proofreader:** Kathy Bennett; **Indexer:** Dan Connolly; **Graphic Designer:** Fred Starbird; **Graphic Artist:** Francine Hamerski; **Cover Designer:** Keith Blomberg; **Photographer (cover):** © Victor Baldizon/NBAE/Getty Images; **Photographer (interior):** Neil Bernstein, unless otherwise noted; **DVD Models:** Udonis Haslem, Rashual Butler, Matt Frieje, Jasmine Obhrai; **Book Models:** Russell McAdoo, Eric Foran, Jasmine Obhrai; **Photo Asset Manager:** Laura Fitch; **Photo Office Assistant:** Jason Allen; **Art Manager:** Kelly Hendren; **Illustrator:** Alan L. Wilborn; **Printer:** United Graphics

We thank the Miami Heat in Miami, Florida, for assistance in providing the location for the photo shoot for this book.

Human Kinetics books are available at special discounts for bulk purchase. Special editions or book excerpts can also be created to specification. For details, contact the Special Sales Manager at Human Kinetics.

Printed in the United States of America   10 9 8 7 6 5 4 3 2 1

Human Kinetics
Web site: www.HumanKinetics.com

United States: Human Kinetics
P.O. Box 5076
Champaign, IL 61825-5076
800-747-4457
e-mail: humank@hkusa.com

Canada: Human Kinetics
475 Devonshire Road Unit 100
Windsor, ON N8Y 2L5
800-465-7301 (in Canada only)
e-mail: orders@hkcanada.com

Europe: Human Kinetics
107 Bradford Road
Stanningley
Leeds LS28 6AT, United Kingdom
+44 (0) 113 255 5665
e-mail: hk@hkeurope.com

Australia: Human Kinetics
57A Price Avenue
Lower Mitcham, South Australia 5062
08 8372 0999
e-mail: info@hkaustralia.com

New Zealand: Human Kinetics
Division of Sports Distributors NZ Ltd.
P.O. Box 300 226 Albany
North Shore City
Auckland
0064 9 448 1207
e-mail: info@humankinetics.co.nz

Contents

DVD Contents

Fitness Tests

No-Step Vertical Jump

Maximum Vertical Jump

Lane Agility

Three-Quarter-Court Sprint

Conditioning Drills

Full-Court Sprint Dribble

Full-Court Sprint With Chest Pass

Full-Court Sprint With Bounce Pass

Full-Court Sprint With One Touch Pass

Angled Sideline Sprint Layup

Half-Court Sprint, Elbow Jump Shot

Core Exercises

Medicine Ball Sit-Up Toss

Leg Raise Circle

Leg Thrust

Hanging Knee-Up

Hanging Knee-Up With a Medicine Ball

Hanging Straight-Leg Raise

Half Bicycle

Hanging Diagonal Raise

Medicine Ball Touches

Swiss Ball Back Extension

Medicine Ball Partner Over–Under

Straight-Leg Deadlift (Two Feet, One Dumbbell)

Straight-Leg Deadlift (One Foot, Two Dumbbells)

Swiss Ball Reverse Hyperextension

Reverse Hyperextension

Swiss Ball Alternating Superman

Four-Way Stabilization With Movement–Prone

Four-Way Stabilization With Movement–Supine

Four-Way Stabilization With Movement–Side

Strength Exercises

Squat

Hang Pull

Hang Clean

Power Clean

Straight-Leg Deadlift

Step-Up

Combo Lift (Hang Clean, Front Squat, Push Press, Straight-Leg Deadlift)

Lunge

Side Lunge

Back Extension

Power Plyometric Exercises

Double-Leg Diagonal Barrier Jump

Double-Leg Hop

Knees-to-Chest Jump

Side-to-Side Box Jump

Depth Jump

Box Circuit

Power Skip

Bound

Single-Leg Spring-Up

Alternating Power Jump

Double-Leg Side-to-Side

Single-Leg Side-to-Side

Single-Leg Diagonal

Quick-Step Box Touch

Lateral Box Quick Feet

Medicine Ball Bounce Pass

Medicine Ball Overhead Pass

Medicine Ball Drop

Double-Leg Power Dunk or Layup

Agility Exercises

Hip Rotation

Icky Shuffle

Crossover Icky Shuffle

Skier

Shuffle, Shuffle, Sprint

Five-Spot Closeout

Partner Five-Spot Closeout

Total Running Time . . . . **60 minutes**

Foreword

I am pleased to have the opportunity to endorse and recommend *Complete Conditioning for Basketball* to you. The conditioning coaches in the NBA have a special expertise and do a tremendous job with their respective teams. In this book, their organization, the NBCCA, shares its collective knowledge on how to best develop and hone the athleticism of basketball players.

Mike Brundgardt, the only strength and conditioning coach the Spurs have ever had, has been invaluable to our basketball team winning multiple titles during his tenure. Mike and the other conditioning coaches in the league understand not only all the anatomical structures, biomechanical aspects, and scheduling considerations associated with training for the sport, they also know the game, and what specifically it takes in the way of physical preparation to excel on the court. No, a conditioning coach isn't the one to consult for improving shooting technique, but he very well might help develop the upper body strength or leg power to make a player's shooting motion more effortless, fluid, and effective.

Much has changed in athlete conditioning since I received my master's degree in physical education and sports science at the University of Denver, while also serving as an assistant basketball coach at the U.S. Air Force Academy. Better equipment, better nutrition, well, pretty much better everything. But from a coach's standpoint, the best innovations of all are those that have tailored the training process to meet the demands of the game, and even individual physical and positional needs. The next time you see one of the old "classic" games from the '60s or '70s, note how much smaller, slower, and less powerful the athletes were, in general, compared to today's amazing physical specimens.

Complete Conditioning for Basketball presents all the latest, proven methods for taking a player's game to the next level through superior physical training. Individuals and teams that follow the advice and use the drills, exercises, and programs recommended in this book and DVD will be a step ahead of the competition—and just maybe, on the way to a championship season.

Gregg Popovich
Head Coach, San Antonio Spurs

Basketball Conditioning Essentials

It is easy to see how basketball players have changed over the last 30 years. They are bigger, stronger, and more powerful than the players of the 1970s and '80s. The reason is the total conditioning programs that players follow on almost a year-round basis. In *Complete Conditioning for Basketball*, 11 NBA strength and conditioning coaches use the latest in sport-specific drills and exercises to create the optimal conditioning program for basketball.

Complete conditioning for basketball includes all the components covered in this book: strength, power, agility, speed, quickness, flexibility, and anaerobic conditioning. The drills and exercises are for both male and female basketball players. There are workout programs for all levels, from a beginner's first workout to advanced programs for NBA and WNBA players.

Each June the NBA strength and conditioning coaches test the top 80 to 100 potential draft picks at the Predraft Combine in Chicago. These performance tests measure strength, speed, power, agility, and flexibility. In chapter 1, Tests and Evaluation, these tests are explained in detail. Both male and female athletes at the professional, college, high school level, and junior high school level can perform each of the performance tests that are used at the NBA Predraft Combine. This chapter also has the results from the last 5 years of testing at the predraft combine, including the maximum, minimum, and averages of each test plus position averages. Test results for high school athletes, both male and female, and college female athletes are included.

Chapter 2, Warm-Up and Flexibility, includes a dynamic warm-up specific for basketball and an innovative way of stretching called active isolated stretching. Active isolated stretching involves movement and really gets you ready for practices and games. Improved flexibility will help improve performance and reduce injuries. The 20 stretches that cover the total body are explained in detail.

Conditioning for basketball is one component, but it may be the most important component. You must be in great shape to reach your full potential. Chapter 3, Conditioning, includes the 12-Week Off-Season Conditioning Program, which will develop your basketball conditioning and your recovery systems so you will be in great shape for the first day of practice. Included are track workouts, basketball court drills, and court conditioning circuits that will improve your conditioning and your game at the same time.

The development of functional strength will improve your power and speed and make you a better athlete and basketball player. Chapter 4, Strength, includes a detailed explanation of the fundamentals of strength training. This will give you the basic knowledge to start a proper strength training program safely. Included are two Off-Season Strength Training Programs; a Four-Day Split Program, and a Three-Day Total-Body Program. Five in-season strength training program options are explained for good variety over the course of a long season. Every functional strength training exercise is explained in detail with proper and safe technique.

Core strength has become more important over the past few years. The 34 functional exercises specifically for the core are included in 6 categories. The categories are trunk flexion, hip flexion, and rotary torso for the abdominals and trunk extension, hip extension, and total-core stabilization for the lower back.

Plyometric drills are performed to help athletes increase power. Power is the combination of speed and strength. Increased power helps speed, strength, agility, quickness, and jumping ability. In chapter 5, Power, the 33 plyometric drills are included in 5 categories: double-leg drills, single-leg drills, quick-feet drills, upper-body drills, and sport-specific drills.

Any basketball player will be a better athlete with increased speed. Speed can give you an advantage both offensively and defensively in full-court as well as half-court game situations. The 18 speed development drills in chapter 6 are explained and categorized in beginning, intermediate, and advanced drills. The beginning and intermediate drills focus on proper running mechanics. The advanced speed drills include resistance speed training drills and assistance overspeed training drills.

Agility is the ability to change direction quickly, explosively, and under control. Basketball players who can do this have a great advantage. Stops, starts, changes of direction, turns and cuts, and defensive shuffles are all agility movements performed many times during practices and games. The 20 agility drills in chapter 7 include ladder drills, minihurdle drills, cone drills, and court drills.

Atlanta Hawks guard Joe Johnson shoots over New York Knicks center Eddy Curry. A basketball player uses all his skills—flexibility, conditioning, strength, power, speed, and agility—to get the ball to the hoop.

© Erik S. Lesser/epa/Corbis

An important area that is not covered in the scope of this book is nutrition. You must make nutrition a high priority if you want to be at your best. Energy for performance as well as recovery from tough workouts comes from proper nutrition.

The complete conditioning schedule in chapter 8 explains both daily workouts and the 12-Week Complete Conditioning program. The sample daily workouts show you how each component fits into a training program. They will help you organize your training so you can get the most out of it. The 12-Week Complete Conditioning program shows the daily, weekly, and monthly progressions of each component of the training program.

Each of the components covered in this book and DVD will help you to become a better basketball player. When you train and develop all the components, you have a better chance of reaching your potential. Enjoy your training and your improved game!

USING THE DVD

Complete Conditioning for Basketball is a total package. The book and DVD compliment each other to present all the information, tests, drills, and exercises that coaches and players need to create effective workouts and programs. Use the book to learn the importance of each component of conditioning—testing, flexibility, aerobic conditioning, strength, power, speed, and agility. Apply the information from the book to create training programs that will produce results on the court. Watch the DVD to see the more complicated exercises in action. Learn the proper technique for the more complex and dynamic tests, drills, lifts, and plyometric exercises.

Key to Diagrams

⟶	Direction of movement
▲	Cone
Ⓢ	Shot
Ⓙ	Jump
C	Coach
P	Player
P/R	Passer/rebounder
T	Timer
L	Left foot
R	Right foot

Chapter 1

Tests and Evaluation

Testing and performance assessment tools are important in the overall evaluation of athletes and provide feedback on the effectiveness of the speed, strength, power, agility, and flexibility programs used. Effective testing procedures include the following:

1. Developing and using standardized norms and numbers
2. Using proven tests that have been repeated several times
3. Creating your own testing procedures that are safe and effective and that accurately measure what you intend to measure

The testing results provide direct comparisons between current athletes and athletes who have previously been tested. Data collected also allow the coach to make changes in the program to improve the quality of the program. By continually examining the program and the athletes involved, coaches are able to change and improve the program. These evolving improvements help to solidify and strengthen the assessments of the athletes in the program.

Our focus was to determine which information would be the most beneficial to coaches and athletes at all levels of basketball—NBA, WNBA, college, and high school—and both male and female players. The data that we have collected present many possible comparisons for coaches and athletes to use and will assist coaches with the direction and development of training programs. The testing results will also help motivate athletes to train to be better basketball players.

NBA PREDRAFT TESTING

Once the NBA season is complete, each team begins its final preparation for draft day. Before the creation of the Chicago Predraft Combine, athletes from all over the world traveled to each team's facility and were given individual workouts that consisted of several tests. The tests may include psychological testing, individual meetings with the general managers and coaches, and basketball workouts. The basketball workouts were often composed of shooting drills, ball-handling drills, defensive drills, and 1-on-1, 2-on-2, or even 3-on-3 games. During this time, strength and conditioning coaches also conducted anthropometric measurements and performance testing on each athlete. This testing often included the following:

- Height, with and without shoes
- Body weight (measured while players were wearing shorts only)
- Standing reach (with shoes)
- Wingspan
- Percentage of body fat
- Lower-body power
- Lower-body strength
- Upper-body strength
- Speed
- Agility
- Balance
- Eye–hand coordination

NBA team visits by potential draft picks often took 3 to 6 hours for each athlete. Every potential draft pick was faced with the daunting task of performing at his highest level every time he arrived in a new NBA city.

Athletes' travel schedules were grueling. They might travel to 8 to 10 workouts in a 10- to 14-day period, and each team conducted a 1- to 2-hour basketball workout session in addition to any performance and physical assessment tests the team deemed necessary. Athletes traveled to each city and endured 8 straight days of lower-body strength testing, upper-body strength testing, lower-body power testing, agility testing, and speed testing, and each of those tests might have been different in each city. Imagine 8 to 10 straight days of the bench press, leg press or squat, vertical jumps, agility tests, and sprints.

These types of tests were combined with some of the most intense individual basketball workouts that the athletes might ever encounter. Athletes often arrived at their NBA workouts unable to perform at their highest level. Their legs, lower backs, chests, and arms were sore and fatigued from previous workouts conducted in the other NBA cities they had visited. That did not allow athletes to perform to the best of their abilities. The bottom line is that the athletes must be able to perform basketball skills to their highest level each time they step on the court.

This grueling travel schedule and the array of basketball workouts and physical testing were the driving force behind the development of standardized performance testing at the Chicago Predraft Combine. Standardized performance testing was first performed in Chicago in June 2000.

IDENTIFICATION AND DEVELOPMENT OF TESTING CATEGORIES

For strength and conditioning coaches at the NBA, college, or high school levels, the challenge is to develop standardized tests that meet the needs of the team and evaluate the physical measurements, fitness levels, and athletic performance of athletes. Conducting a pretest before starting the training program and a posttest after completing the training program is critical for evaluating the effectiveness of the program. Knowing where athletes rank compared to their peers helps to motivate and drive athletes to improve their performance. The following performance categories were identified as the most appropriate on which to acquire baseline data and were performed in this order:

1. Lower-body power
2. Agility
3. Speed
4. Upper-body strength
5. Flexibility

A major concern when developing the categories of baseline tests is to ensure the primary requirements of testing—validity and reliability—were followed with each assessment.

Validity is an estimate of the extent to which a test measures what it was designed to measure. For example, does the Three-Quarter-Court Sprint truly measure speed? To what degree does it measure speed?

Reliability refers to the extent to which a test consistently measures a given factor. In order for the test to be reliable, the test being conducted must be consistently repeated in the same manner for each athlete, from test to test. For example, using the same protocol for timing and recording the times in the same way is crucial to the reliability of the test and the data collected.

PERFORMANCE TESTS

These tests can be adjusted to fit the level of each athlete. For example, the Lane Agility drill and the Three-Quarter-Court Sprint should be performed on the appropriate regulation court for each player's level. High school males should bench press 135 pounds (about 61 kilograms) instead of 185 pounds (about 84 kilograms). If a Vertec machine is not available, a backboard or wall may be used to test the No-Step and Maximum Vertical Jumps.

Test relevance was also a major factor in our developmental process. The tests we incorporated help identify areas in which athletes can improve. These areas have a direct relevance to the overall effectiveness of the athletes' game. Once the physiological categories for testing were identified, the National Basketball Conditioning Coaches Association (NBCCA) testing committee developed relevant, reliable, and valid tests that we believed were appropriate. The tests listed in table 1.1 were selected to help identify athletic qualities as they directly relate to basketball performance at any level—professional, college, or high school—and for both male and female players.

These tests were selected because they match the physical qualities associated with optimal basketball performance. These tests also supply baseline information involving the primary areas of athletic testing. The tests are easily replicable, are reliable, and are directly related to the physical qualities necessary for performing at a high level on the basketball court. Does the No-Step Vertical Jump truly measure lower-body power? Will the Lane Agility drill test various changes in speed and direction that are required in basketball activities? Does the Three-Quarter-Court Sprint measure all-out speed, which is often used during transitions from offense to defense? Finally, will the Bench Press test give a good indication of upper-body strength, a quality that is becoming more important in modern basketball? These tests match the questions we posed during the development of the testing battery.

The next step was to bring together a testing protocol that could easily be repeated and used on any basketball court. (The Bench Press and Sit-and-Reach may be tested in the weight room or other areas.)

Table 1.1 Tests for Specific Performance Categories

Performance categories	Tests
Lower-body power	No-Step Vertical Jump Maximum Vertical Jump
Agility and quickness	Lane Agility
Speed	Three-Quarter-Court Sprint
Upper-body strength	Bench Press (maximum repetitions)*
Flexibility	Sit-and-Reach

* For the Bench Press, NBA and male college players press 185 pounds (84 kg). Male high school players press 135 pounds (61 kg). WNBA and female college players press 95 pounds (43 kg). Female high school players press 75 pounds (34 kg).

Performance Testing Protocol—High School, College, WNBA, and NBA

Before starting the performance testing, always warm up and stretch for 10 to 15 minutes. The rest intervals between tests should be at least 2 minutes. Perform all the tests in the proper order:

1. No-Step Vertical Jump
2. Maximum Vertical Jump
3. Lane Agility
4. Three-Quarter-Court Sprint (baseline to opposite foul line)
5. Bench Press (maximum repetitions)
6. Sit-and-Reach

To protect the health of the players and the integrity of the testing, follow these safety guidelines:

- Make sure players engage in a proper warm-up before beginning testing.
- Only coaches and players are allowed in the testing area—no bystanders.
- Players should be properly supervised in all areas at all times.
- Before testing, players should receive proper instruction and a demonstration of each test.

PERFORMANCE TESTS

Test 1: No-Step Vertical Jump

Equipment: Vertec machine, backboard, or wall

1. Measure standing reach, in shoes, on the Vertec or wall. Stand with both feet flat on the ground, legs and torso straight. Reach up with a straight arm, wrist, and hand. With your fingers, touch at the highest point.

2. Jump straight up as high as possible and, with a straight arm, tap the Vertec device or mark the wall at the highest point (figure 1.1). No shuffle steps, side steps, drop steps, or gather steps are allowed.

3. Make two attempts. If, on the second attempt, you reach a higher height, a third attempt is awarded.

4. The vertical jump is the difference, in inches, between the standing reach and the jump reach.

Figure 1.1

DVD Test 2: Maximum Vertical Jump

Equipment: Vertec machine, backboard, or wall

1. Measure standing reach, in shoes, on the Vertec or wall. Stand with both feet flat on the ground. Torso and legs are straight. Reach up with a straight arm, wrist, hand, fingers touching at the highest point.

2. Maximum approach distance is measured from the free-throw line extended in a 15-foot (4.6 m) arc to the baseline.

3. Take as many steps toward the Vertec, backboard, or wall as necessary to acquire a maximum vertical jump. Everyone is required to start within the 15-foot arc, and each athlete has the choice of a one- or two-foot takeoff.

4. Make two attempts. If on the second attempt you reach a higher height, a third attempt is rewarded.

5. The vertical jump is the difference, in inches, between the standing reach and the jump reach.

DVD Test 3: Lane Agility

Equipment: Basketball lane, 4 cones, a stopwatch, floor tape to mark the start and finish line and the change-of-direction line

1. Place cones on each of the 4 corners of the lane (figure 1.2).

2. Start at the left-hand corner of the free-throw line facing the baseline. Sprint to the baseline, go past the cone and defensive-shuffle to the right corner of the lane and past the cone, backpedal to the free-throw line past the cone, defensive-shuffle to the left, and touch the change-of-direction line with your left foot. Then change direction back to your right, defensive shuffle to the right past the cone at the right-hand corner of free-throw line, sprint to the baseline past the cone, defensive-shuffle to the left past the cone at the left-hand corner of the lane, and backpedal past the starting position through the finish line.

3. Two attempts are allowed; take the faster time of the two. One foul is allowed without penalty, and you are given the chance to start over. A

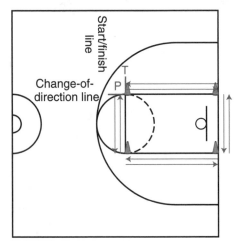

Figure 1.2

foul includes moving or knocking down a cone, cutting a corner of the drill, sprinting sideways instead of defensive-shuffling, crossing your feet, not touching the change-of-direction line, or falling down.

4. Timing begins on your first movement.

Test 4: Three-Quarter-Court Sprint

Equipment: Gym floor, 4 cones, a stopwatch, and a wall pad if necessary

1. Place 2 cones at the baseline and free-throw lane lines. Place 2 cones at the elbows of the opposite free-throw line (figure 1.3). For safety, place crash pads against the wall at the end of the three-quarter-court sprint.

2. Start with a two-point stance with your front foot behind the edge of the baseline.

3. The timing begins on your first movement. Sprint through the opposite free-throw line.

4. Two attempts are allowed. Take the faster of the two.

Figure 1.3

Test 5: Bench Press (Maximum Repetitions)

Equipment: Bench press bench, Olympic barbell, weights, and collars (secure collars on barbell before lifting)

1. Warm up. Perform 10 push-ups, followed by a 60-second rest. Bench press the warm-up weight for 5 repetitions. NBA and male college players lift 135 pounds (61 kilograms), male high school players

lift 95 pounds (43 kilograms), WNBA and female college players lift 65 pounds (29 kilograms), and female high school players lift 45 pounds (20 kilograms).

2. Rest for 90 seconds. Prepare for the bench press. You will bench press the appropriate weight for the maximum number of repetitions you can perform. NBA and male college players press 185 pounds (84 kilograms), male high school players press 135 pounds (61 kilograms), WNBA and female college players press 95 pounds (43 kilograms), and female high school players press 75 pounds (34 kilograms).

3. Lie on the weight bench. Grasp the barbell with a grip slightly wider than shoulder width (figure 1.4a) and lower the weight until the barbell touches your chest (figure 1.4b).

4. Push the bar upward until elbows are fully extended. This counts as 1 repetition. Keep upper back and gluteals on the bench the entire time. Keep feet planted on the floor.

5. Two spotters are needed. One spotter provides a lift off the rack, counts the number of repetitions, and makes sure that each repetition is fully locked out at the top and touches the chest at the bottom. The other spotter watches to make sure the gluteals stay in contact with the bench (no arching).

6. You have 1 attempt to complete a maximum number of repetitions. The maximum number of repetitions is recorded.

Figure 1.4

Test 6: Sit-and-Reach Flexibility

Equipment: Sit-and-reach testing device or a yardstick taped to the floor

1. Remove your shoes and test in socks or bare feet. Place your feet on the front side of the measuring device or at the 12-inch (30 cm) mark if using a yardstick or meter stick.

2. Place the fingers of 1 hand on top of the other. Lock the knees out and reach forward onto the measuring device and hold for 1 second (figure 1.5). The spotter may hold the knees down flat on the floor if necessary.

3. Each athlete is given 2 attempts to measure maximum lower-back and hamstring flexibility. Scores are recorded in plus or minus inches or centimeters. Reaching past the feet is plus; not reaching the feet is minus.

Figure 1.5

Test Results and Interpretation

Each athlete's results from these physical assessment tests can be compared to the appropriate player samples in tables 1.2 through 1.9. A large database has been compiled that includes athletes, both male and female, from high school, college, and professional basketball teams. The test results from the NBA Predraft Combine show the full battery of tests.

Table 1.2 Test Results for Elite High School Males and Females

Categories	Scoring	Elite high school males				
		1s Point guards	2s Shooting guards	3s Small forwards	4s Power forwards	5s Centers
Player height without shoes (ft./in.)	Maximum	6' 2.75"	6' 7"	6' 7"	6' 9"	7' 2"
	Average	5' 11.5"	6' 2.5"	6' 4.5"	6' 7.5"	6' 8.5"
	Minimum	5' 6.75"	5' 11"	6' 1.75"	6' 4"	6' 6"
Player weight (lbs.)	Maximum	195.0	209.0	256.0	256.0	300.0
	Average	168.0	187.3	201.0	220.0	225.5
	Minimum	141.0	170.0	168.0	189.0	177.0
Wingspan (ft./in.)	Maximum	6' 10"	6' 10.5"	7' 1.5"	7' 3.5"	8' 0"
	Average	6' 3.5"	6' 6.25"	6' 8"	6' 11.5"	7' 0.5"
	Minimum	5' 11"	6' 1.5"	6' 5.5"	6' 7.5"	6' 8.5"
Standing reach (ft./in.)	Maximum	8' 6.5"	8' 7"	8' 8.5"	8' 11"	9' 9.5"
	Average	7' 11.4"	8' 4.5"	8' 6.2"	8' 8.9"	8' 11.1"
	Minimum	7' 6.5"	7' 9.5"	8' 0"	8' 6.5"	8' 6.5"
No-Step Vertical Jump (in.)	Maximum	32.00	32.00	32.00	30.50	33.00
	Average	28.50	28.00	28.00	26.50	26.75
	Minimum	26.00	23.50	25.50	23.50	23.00
Maximum Vertical Jump (in.)	Maximum	39.0	37.0	38.5	34.0	35.5
	Average	33.5	32.5	33.0	30.5	30.0
	Minimum	27.5	29.0	27.5	25.5	22.5
Lane Agility (sec.)	Maximum	12.67	12.6	12.8	13.6	13.64
	Average	11.62	11.82	11.92	12.37	12.89
	Minimum	10.8	10.92	11.8	11.21	11.3
Three-Quarter-Court Sprint (sec.)	Maximum	3.4	3.5	3.56	3.78	3.91
	Average	3.26	3.33	3.38	3.5	3.48
	Minimum	3.09	3.06	3.23	3.19	3.18
Bench Press (maximum repetitions)	Maximum	25	24	27	28	24
	Average	11	10.3	13.8	13.7	12
	Minimum	0	0	6	0	0
Categories	Scoring	Elite high school females				
		1s Point guards	2s Shooting guards	3s Small forwards	4s Power forwards	5s Centers
No-Step Vertical Jump (in.)	Maximum	20.0	21.0	20.0	21.0	19.0
	Average	16.0	19.0	18.0	17.0	16.5
	Minimum	13.0	15.0	16.5	15.5	15.0
Maximum Vertical Jump (in.)	Maximum	24.0	24.0	23.0	24.0	22.0
	Average	17.0	22.0	21.5	19.5	19.5
	Minimum	15.0	17.0	18.0	18.5	17.0
Lane Agility (sec.)	Maximum	12.49	12.46	12.55	12.67	13.80
	Average	11.99	11.89	12.00	12.21	12.86
	Minimum	11.34	11.56	11.75	11.80	12.00
Three-Quarter-Court Sprint (sec.)	Maximum	3.70	3.77	3.80	4.00	4.08
	Average	3.60	3.65	3.62	3.82	3.87
	Minimum	3.57	3.43	3.48	3.75	3.72
Bench Press (maximum repetitions)	Maximum	12	10	13	15	15
	Average	9	8	8	12	11
	Minimum	5	6	7	9	8

Data on elite high school males gathered at NBA Players Association high school combine.

English-to-metric conversions: To convert inches to centimeters, multiply number of inches by 2.540005. To convert feet to meters, multiply number of feet by .3048006. To convert feet to centimeters, multiply number of feet by 30.48006.

Table 1.3 Test Results for NCAA Division I Players

Males					
Player	No-Step Vertical Jump (in.)	Maximum Vertical Jump (in.)	Lane Agility (sec.)	Three-Quarter-Court Sprint (sec.)	Bench Press (maximum repetitions)
1	32.5	37.5	9.83	3.30	18
2	25.5	30.0	10.98	3.67	7
3	30.5	32.5	10.82	3.67	14
4	32.5	39.5	10.35	3.37	12
5	29.0	36.0	9.72	3.34	12
6	26.0	28.0	11.43	3.60	9
7	25.5	28.5	10.47	3.51	4
8	31.0	38.5	9.60	3.26	13
9	25.5	30.0	10.58	3.60	10
10	33.5	39.0	9.45	3.20	13
11	22.5	27.0	10.45	3.51	0
12	28.5	33.5	9.84	3.62	14
13	29.5	36.0	9.88	3.39	5
14	28.5	34.5	10.01	3.42	9
Average	28.5	33.0	10.24	3.46	10

Females					
Player	No-Step Vertical Jump (in.)	Maximum Vertical Jump (in.)	Lane Agility (sec.)	Three-Quarter-Court Sprint (sec.)	Bench Press (maximum repetitions)
1	25.0	26.5	12.00	3.66	9
2	20.5	21.0	11.85	3.90	23
3	20.5	21.0	11.96	4.00	26
4	20.5	25.0	11.18	3.72	Injured
5	17.5	22.0	12.01	3.97	11
6	23.0	27.5	11.90	3.80	10
7	23.0	31.5	10.76	3.51	10
8	Injured	Injured	Injured	Injured	31
9	20.5	24.5	11.21	3.84	11
10	24.5	29.5	11.74	3.86	Injured
Average	22.1	25.2	11.62	3.81	17.8

English-to-metric conversions: To convert inches to centimeters, multiply number of inches by 2.540005. To convert feet to meters, multiply number of feet by .3048006. To convert feet to centimeters, multiply number of feet by 30.48006.

Table 1.4 Test Results for WNBA Players

Position	Scoring	No-Step Vertical Jump (in.)	Maximum Vertical Jump (in.)	Lane Agility (sec.)	Three-Quarter-Court Sprint (sec.)	Bench Press (maximum repetitions)
1s Point guards	Maximum	24.0	26.0	12.60	3.70	20
	Average	22.0	24.5	11.91	3.57	16
	Minimum	19.0	23.0	11.22	3.45	12
2s Shooting guards	Maximum	23.0	25.0	12.49	3.65	25
	Average	21.5	23.0	12.02	3.54	20.5
	Minimum	20.0	22.0	11.56	3.43	16
3s Small forwards	Maximum	23.5	25.0	12.20	3.75	26
	Average	21.5	23.0	11.69	3.62	20
	Minimum	19.5	21.0	11.19	3.50	14
4s Power forwards	Maximum	21.5	24.0	12.42	3.74	25
	Average	20.0	22.0	12.21	3.63	17
	Minimum	18.5	20.0	12.00	3.53	9
5s Centers	Maximum	21.0	23.0	13.76	4.08	22
	Average	18.5	21.0	12.86	3.85	15.5
	Minimum	16.5	19.0	11.98	3.62	9

English-to-metric conversions: To convert inches to centimeters, multiply number of inches by 2.540005. To convert feet to meters, multiply number of feet by .3048006. To convert feet to centimeters, multiply number of feet by 30.48006.

Table 1.5 NBA Predraft Camp Testing Results 2002 to 2006: 1s—Point Guards

Categories	Scoring	2002	2003	2004	2005	2006
Player height without shoes (ft./in.)	Maximum	6' 3"	6' 6"	6' 6.5"	6' 2.5"	6' 5.75"
	Average	6' 0.52"	6' 1.73"	6' 1.25"	6' 0.3"	6' 1.58"
	Minimum	5' 8"	5' 9.75"	5' 7.5"	5' 9.25"	5' 9"
Player weight (lbs.)	Maximum	212.00	217.00	223.00	202.40	224.00
	Average	184.55	189.29	189.00	182.07	193.33
	Minimum	155.00	162.00	170.00	154.40	165.00
Wingspan (ft./in.)	Maximum	6' 10"	6' 11"	6' 11"	6' 10"	6' 11.25"
	Average	6' 3.93"	6' 5.54"	6' 6"	6' 4.07"	6' 6.11"
	Minimum	5' 10.75"	5' 11.5"	5' 11.5"	5' 11.5"	6' 0.75"
Standing reach (ft./in.)	Maximum	8' 11.5"	8' 7.5"	8' 11"	8' 4.5"	8' 8"
	Average	8' 1.28"	8' 2.02"	8' 2.25"	8' 0.02"	8' 1.57"
	Minimum	7' 6.5"	7' 8"	7' 7.5"	7' 8"	7' 8.5"
No-Step Vertical Jump (in.)	Maximum	33.00	37.50	37.00	33.00	35.00
	Average	27.63	29.86	29.00	29.28	30.40
	Minimum	21.00	24.50	23.50	24.50	24.50
Maximum Vertical Jump (in.)	Maximum	37.50	41.50	43.50	40.50	42.00
	Average	32.97	35.83	33.68	34.92	35.57
	Minimum	26.50	29.50	28.50	28.50	28.50
Lane Agility (sec.)	Maximum	12.46	12.17	11.80	12.13	12.00
	Average	11.50	11.25	11.11	11.04	11.22
	Minimum	10.34	10.62	10.45	10.44	10.35
Three-Quarter-Court Sprint (sec.)	Maximum	3.39	3.42	3.34	3.38	3.43
	Average	3.22	3.20	3.19	3.22	3.25
	Minimum	3.03	3.06	2.96	3.00	3.08
Bench Press (maximum repetitions)	Maximum	24	17	15	15	19
	Average	7.95	8.24	8.94	8.78	9.86
	Minimum	0	0	1	0	1.0
Sit-and-Reach (in.)	Maximum	11.50	9.50	7.50	6.25	NT
	Average	4.50	4.50	4.25	2.16	NT
	Minimum	−4.00	−1.00	1.50	−3.50	NT

English-to-metric conversions: To convert inches to centimeters, multiply number of inches by 2.540005. To convert feet to meters, multiply number of feet by .3048006. To convert feet to centimeters, multiply number of feet by 30.48006.

NT = Not tested

Table 1.6 NBA Predraft Camp Testing Results 2002 to 2006: 2s—Shooting Guards

Categories	Scoring	2002	2003	2004	2005	2006
Player height without shoes (ft./in.)	Maximum	6' 7"	6' 7.25"	6' 7"	6' 6.25"	6' 5.75"
	Average	6' 3.64"	6' 3.95"	6' 4.05"	6' 3.06"	6' 3.39"
	Minimum	6' 0"	5' 11.5"	6' 0.05"	5' 10.5"	5' 11.75"
Player weight (lbs.)	Maximum	222.00	245.00	228.00	223.20	224.00
	Average	200.08	204.69	205.00	192.70	206.90
	Minimum	167.00	165.00	181.00	165.20	175.00
Wingspan (ft./in.)	Maximum	7' 1.5"	7' 2"	7' 2"	7' 1"	7' 0"
	Average	6' 8.42"	6' 7.89"	6' 9.5"	6' 7.96"	6' 7.53"
	Minimum	6' 2"	6' 4"	6' 6"	5' 11.75"	6' 0.75"
Standing reach (ft./in.)	Maximum	8' 11.5"	8' 10.25"	8' 11.5"	8' 11.5"	8' 8"
	Average	8' 6.02"	8' 4.85"	8' 6.46"	8' 5.02"	8' 3.68"
	Minimum	8' 0"	7' 10.5"	8' 2"	7' 9"	7' 8.5"
No-Step Vertical Jump (in.)	Maximum	33.50	37.50	37.00	33.00	37.50
	Average	27.74	29.46	29.28	28.75	30.28
	Minimum	21.00	23.50	24.00	24.50	27.00
Maximum Vertical Jump (in.)	Maximum	38.00	41.50	43.50	40.50	41.50
	Average	32.69	34.89	34.34	33.33	35.87
	Minimum	28.50	29.50	30.00	29.00	31.50
Lane Agility (sec.)	Maximum	12.30	12.19	11.95	12.13	12.00
	Average	11.46	11.26	11.22	11.12	11.23
	Minimum	10.78	10.44	10.70	10.32	10.35
Three-Quarter-Court Sprint (sec.)	Maximum	3.39	3.38	3.38	3.41	3.48
	Average	3.23	3.20	3.21	3.25	3.26
	Minimum	3.03	3.04	3.10	3.00	3.06
Bench Press (maximum repetitions)	Maximum	24	18	19	17	20
	Average	8.48	10.13	11.39	8.40	11.13
	Minimum	0	0	1	0	1
Sit-and-Reach (in.)	Maximum	12	12	9.50	7.50	NT
	Average	6	4.5	4.32	3.74	NT
	Minimum	−2.5	−1.0	0	−3.5	NT

English-to-metric conversions: To convert inches to centimeters, multiply number of inches by 2.540005. To convert feet to meters, multiply number of feet by .3048006. To convert feet to centimeters, multiply number of feet by 30.48006.

NT = Not tested

Table 1.7   NBA Predraft Camp Testing Results 2002 to 2006: 3s—Small Forwards

Categories	Scoring	2002	2003	2004	2005	2006
Player height without shoes (ft./in.)	Maximum	6' 8.25"	6' 10"	6' 10.25"	6' 10"	6' 8"
	Average	6' 6.08"	6' 7.04"	6' 6.77"	6' 6.16"	6' 5.74"
	Minimum	6' 3.5"	6' 3.75"	6' 3.5"	6' 2.25"	6' 2"
Player weight (lbs.)	Maximum	255.00	246.00	263.00	252.40	238.00
	Average	214.35	222.70	221.50	215.17	215.42
	Minimum	193.00	200.00	193.00	186.60	179.00
Wingspan (ft./in.)	Maximum	7' 1.75"	7' 4.25"	7' 3.5"	7' 3.5"	7' 3"
	Average	6' 10.97"	6' 10.78"	6' 11.53"	6' 11.25"	6' 10.46"
	Minimum	6' 6.25"	6' 5.25"	6' 7"	6' 7.5"	6' 6.25"
Standing reach (ft./in.)	Maximum	9' 1"	9' 1"	9' 2"	9' 2"	9' 0"
	Average	8' 8.44"	8' 8.77"	8' 9.98"	8' 9.37"	8' 7.03"
	Minimum	8' 0.5"	8' 1"	8' 4"	8' 5"	8' 2.5"
No-Step Vertical Jump (in.)	Maximum	35.50	37.50	33.50	33.50	37.50
	Average	28.76	29.34	28.00	28.50	30.46
	Minimum	24.00	23.50	23.50	22.00	24.50
Maximum Vertical Jump (in.)	Maximum	40.50	41.50	39.50	39.50	41.50
	Average	33.50	34.11	32.45	33.02	35.54
	Minimum	28.50	29.00	26.00	27.00	30.50
Lane Agility (sec.)	Maximum	12.85	12.18	13.08	12.12	12.23
	Average	11.60	11.27	11.48	11.25	11.32
	Minimum	10.68	10.44	10.79	10.32	10.54
Three-Quarter-Court Sprint (sec.)	Maximum	3.43	3.47	3.42	3.56	3.46
	Average	3.26	3.23	3.26	3.29	3.28
	Minimum	3.09	3.04	3.12	3.05	3.06
Bench Press (maximum repetitions)	Maximum	15	25	19	26	24
	Average	8.8	11.21	10.31	9.93	11.72
	Minimum	0	2	1	0	1
Sit-and-Reach (in.)	Maximum	12	10	9.5	8.5	NT
	Average	5	3	3.7	3.78	NT
	Minimum	−2.5	−8	−3	0	NT

English-to-metric conversions: To convert inches to centimeters, multiply number of inches by 2.540005. To convert feet to meters, multiply number of feet by .3048006. To convert feet to centimeters, multiply number of feet by 30.48006.

NT = Not tested

Table 1.8 NBA Predraft Camp Testing Results 2002 to 2006: 4s—Power Forwards

Categories	Scoring	2002	2003	2004	2005	2006
Player height without shoes (ft./in.)	Maximum	6' 10.25"	6' 11.5"	6' 10.5"	7' 1.25"	6' 10"
	Average	6' 8.12"	6' 8.5"	6' 8.15"	6' 7.99"	6' 7.39"
	Minimum	6' 5.75"	6' 5.75"	6' 6.25"	6' 5"	6' 4.75"
Player weight (lbs.)	Maximum	285.00	316.00	272.00	282.00	285.00
	Average	237.91	240.68	235.50	239.62	238.33
	Minimum	214.00	187.00	193.00	206.20	206.00
Wingspan (ft./in.)	Maximum	7' 5.5"	7' 6.25"	7' 5"	7' 6.75"	7' 4.75"
	Average	7' 0.87"	7' 1.11"	7' 1.01"	7' 1.2"	7' 1.38"
	Minimum	6' 9.75"	6' 7.5"	6' 9.5"	6' 9"	6' 9.5"
Standing reach (ft./in.)	Maximum	9' 4"	9' 3.5"	9' 3.5"	9' 4.5"	9' 2"
	Average	8' 11.53"	8' 11.43"	9' 0.01"	8' 11.53"	8' 9.8"
	Minimum	8' 6"	8' 4.5"	8' 9.5"	8' 7.5"	8' 5"
No-Step Vertical Jump (in.)	Maximum	33.50	34.50	32.00	33.50	35.00
	Average	28.48	28.01	27.31	28.32	29.15
	Minimum	24.00	23.50	22.00	21.50	23.00
Maximum Vertical Jump (in.)	Maximum	39.00	41.00	36.00	39.50	40.50
	Average	32.03	32.67	31.50	32.60	33.12
	Minimum	25.00	26.00	26.00	27.00	26.00
Lane Agility (sec.)	Maximum	14.45	14.01	13.13	13.13	13.70
	Average	11.84	11.77	11.92	11.73	11.66
	Minimum	10.73	10.67	10.75	10.62	10.54
Three-Quarter-Court Sprint (sec.)	Maximum	3.52	3.65	3.63	3.68	3.72
	Average	3.29	3.29	3.31	3.34	3.40
	Minimum	3.16	3.08	3.14	3.17	3.10
Bench Press (maximum repetitions)	Maximum	22	27	22	21	26
	Average	12.7	12.43	11.87	12.66	13.23
	Minimum	6	2	1	0	1
Sit-and-Reach (in.)	Maximum	11	10.5	9.5	8.25	NT
	Average	5	3	3.97	2.96	NT
	Minimum	–2	–13.5	–2	–12	NT

English-to-metric conversions: To convert inches to centimeters, multiply number of inches by 2.540005. To convert feet to meters, multiply number of feet by .3048006. To convert feet to centimeters, multiply number of feet by 30.48006.

NT = Not tested

Table 1.9 NBA Predraft Camp Testing Results 2002 to 2006: 5s—Centers

Categories	Scoring	2002	2003	2004	2005	2006
Player height without shoes (ft./in.)	Maximum	7' 0.75"	7' 3.5"	7' 1.75"	7' 1.25"	7' 1.25"
	Average	6' 9.64"	6' 9.64"	6' 9.4"	6' 9.41"	6' 9.01"
	Minimum	6' 6.25"	6' 6.5"	6' 7"	6' 7"	6' 6.5"
Player weight (lbs.)	Maximum	291.00	334.00	272.00	282.00	285.00
	Average	244.63	263.94	245.44	247.00	246.95
	Minimum	218.00	229.00	218.00	214.00	211.00
Wingspan (ft./in.)	Maximum	7' 7"	7' 8"	7' 5.5"	7' 6.75"	7' 8.5"
	Average	7' 1.37"	7' 2.75"	7' 2.33"	7' 3.05"	7' 2.8"
	Minimum	6' 9.75"	6' 11.75"	6' 11"	6' 10"	6' 10.25"
Standing reach (ft./in.)	Maximum	9' 4"	9' 8"	9' 5"	9' 6"	9' 5"
	Average	9' 1.31"	9' 1.31"	9' 1.65"	9' 1.61"	8' 11.65"
	Minimum	8' 10.5"	8' 10.5"	8' 9.5"	8' 8.5"	8' 5.5"
No-Step Vertical Jump (in.)	Maximum	31.00	33.00	32.00	31.50	32.00
	Average	27.12	26.27	28.47	27.34	28.10
	Minimum	24.00	19.50	21.00	21.50	23.00
Maximum Vertical Jump (in.)	Maximum	34.50	37.00	35.50	36.00	39.00
	Average	30.08	30.70	30.68	31.53	32.05
	Minimum	25.00	22.50	25.00	26.50	26.00
Lane Agility (sec.)	Maximum	14.45	14.01	13.32	13.13	13.70
	Average	12.13	12.17	12.22	12.08	12.00
	Minimum	11.05	11.18	10.75	11.48	11.05
Three-Quarter-Court Sprint (sec.)	Maximum	3.63	3.80	3.63	3.68	3.72
	Average	3.35	3.39	3.39	3.40	3.50
	Minimum	3.16	3.20	3.14	3.25	3.29
Bench Press (maximum repetitions)	Maximum	24	27	22	19	26
	Average	13.60	13.31	12.11	11.88	13.21
	Minimum	7	3	1	0	2
Sit-and-Reach (in.)	Maximum	11	8.5	7.5	8.25	NT
	Average	5	3.5	3.19	3.38	NT
	Minimum	–2	–13.5	1	–5.25	NT

English-to-metric conversions: To convert inches to centimeters, multiply number of inches by 2.540005. To convert feet to meters, multiply number of feet by .3048006. To convert feet to centimeters, multiply number of feet by 30.48006.

NT = Not tested

Once you examine the test results that directly correlate to your specific team, develop a testing profile and analyze your athletes' numbers to determine the areas of improvement necessary for each athlete. Let's look at some sample testing profiles and interpret the sample data. These samples will help you to develop each athlete's profile and program. The results for each sample player are listed in table 1.10.

Table 1.10 Sample Test Results for Three Hypothetical Players

Performance categories	Joe Smith High school Shooting guard	Harry Jones NCAA Point guard	Linda Clark NCAA Small forward
No-Step Vertical Jump (in.)	20"	32"	24"
Maximum Vertical Jump (in.)	24"	35"	28"
Lane Agility (sec.)	12.0	10.75	11.15
Three-Quarter-Court Sprint (sec.)	3.2	3.0	3.5
Bench Press (maximum repetitions)*	20	2	8

* Joe Smith bench pressed 135 pounds (61 kg); Harry Jones bench pressed 185 pounds (84 kg); Linda Clark bench pressed 95 pounds (43 kg).
English-to-metric conversions: To convert inches to centimeters, multiply number of inches by 2.540005. To convert feet to meters, multiply number of feet by .3048006. To convert feet to centimeters, multiply number of feet by 30.48006.

Joe Smith is a high school shooting guard. When compared to the data in table 1.2, Joe's results show that his agility and speed are good and his upper-body strength is very good. His scores for the No-Step Vertical Jump and Maximum Vertical Jump are below average, indicating that Joe needs to improve his lower-body power.

Harry Jones is an NCAA Division I point guard. When compared to the data in table 1.3 (NCAA Division I males), Harry's results show his lower-body power is very good and his speed and agility are excellent. His below-average score on the Bench Press shows that Harry needs to improve his upper-body strength.

Linda Clark is an NCAA Division I small forward. When compared to the data in table 1.3 (NCAA Division I females), Linda's results show she is a very explosive and quick athlete. Her scores are average or above average in every test except for Bench Press, indicating that she needs to improve her upper-body strength.

Conditioning Tests and Results

Conditioning tests are another category of tests that may be used in evaluating players. We will look at two examples of conditioning tests: the 4 × 17s and the 4 × 10s.

CONDITIONING TESTS

Conditioning Test: 4 × 17s

The Seattle Sonics (NBA) and Seattle Storm (WNBA) use 4 × 17s as a conditioning test. Run the width of the basketball court, sideline to sideline, 17 times. Over and back equals two repetitions. Table 1.11 lists the time assigned for each position. Table 1.12 shows the test results.

Rest interval between sets: 2 to 2.5 minutes

Banking time: Each set of 17 that you are able to run under your assigned time will allow you to gain time. For example, if you run the first set of 17 2 seconds faster than your assigned time, you will have 2 seconds in the bank (–2). This applies to any of the sets of the 4 × 17s.

Touching lines: You must touch the sidelines on both sides of the court. Each missed touch will cost you 1 second; 1 second, per miss, will be added to that set.

Incomplete test: If you do not pass the test, you will have 30 minutes of extra conditioning after each practice until the test is passed.

Table 1.11 Times Assigned by Position: 4 × 17s

Positions	Sonics	Storm
1s Point guards	63 sec.	67 sec.
2s Shooting guards	64 sec.	69 sec.
3s Small forwards	64 sec.	69 sec.
4s Power forwards	66 sec.	72 sec.
5s Centers	68 sec.	75 sec.

Table 1.12 Test Results for 4 × 17s

Position	Assigned time (sec.)	Set 1 (sec.)	Set 2 (sec.)	Set 3 (sec.)	Set 4 (sec.)	Banked time (sec.)
Seattle Sonics (NBA)						
1 Point guard	63	57	62	58	68	–7
1 Point guard	63	59	59	60	63	–11
2 Shooting guard	63	60	62	65	69	+4
2 Shooting guard	63	58	56	57	63	–18
3 Small forward	64	59	59	60	65	–13
3 Small forward	64	60	62	64	70	0
4 Power forward	66	57	59	60	63	–25
4 Power forward	66	61	62	65	71	–5
5 Center	67	65	67	70	69	+3
5 Center	67	62	64	65	67	–10
Seattle Storm (WNBA)						
1 Point guard	67	62	64	66	67	–9
1 Point guard	67	61	63	65	64	–15
2 Shooting guard	69	62	65	68	67	–14
2 Shooting guard	69	67	69	70	73	+3
3 Small forward	69	64	68	70	70	–4
3 Small forward	69	63	70	79	80	+16
4 Power forward	72	64	64	65	67	–28
4 Power forward	72	67	67	70	75	–9
5 Center	75	69	72	74	78	–7
5 Center	75	70	70	75	82	–3

Alternative Conditioning Test: 4 × 10s

This test consists of running the full length of the court baseline to baseline 10 times. Down and back is equal to 2 repetitions. The times for 10s are about 3 to 4 seconds less than the position times for a 17 (table 1.13).

Rest interval between sets: 2 to 2.5 minutes

Banking time: Each set of 10 that you are able to run under your assigned time will allow you to gain time. For example, if you run the first set of 10 2 seconds faster than your assigned time, you will have 2 seconds in the bank (–2). This applies to any of the sets of the 4 × 10s.

Touching lines: You must touch the baseline on both ends of the court. Each missed touch will cost you 1 second; 1 second, per miss, will be added to that set.

Incomplete test: If you do not pass the test, you will have 30 minutes of extra conditioning after each practice until the test is passed.

Table 1.13   Times Assigned by Position: 4 × 10s

Positions	Sonics	Storm
1s Point guards	59 sec.	63 sec.
2s Shooting guards	60 sec.	65 sec.
3s Small forwards	60 sec.	65 sec.
4s Power forwards	62 sec.	68 sec.
5s Centers	64 sec.	71 sec.

Conditioning tests are a great way to determine the fitness level of athletes. Be wise in your use of these tests and time of year in which you conduct the tests.

This chapter includes a tremendous amount of data compiled from years of testing in many levels of basketball. Comparing your athletes to the testing data will generate ideas for your training programs that will address the strengths and weaknesses of your athletes. Implementing exercises and drills that match the areas of focus that you have identified will allow your athletes to train with purpose and direction.

Chapter 2

Warm-Up and Flexibility

I n today's competitive world of basketball, athletes need every edge, no matter how small. That edge might be an effective warm-up and stretching routine. Often overlooked by some coaches and many athletes, a proper warm-up and stretching routine increases the flexibility of muscles and develops a greater range of motion in the joints, which will lead to improved athletic performance and fewer injuries.

An effective warm-up and stretching routine will improve performance by increasing power, speed, and quickness. These qualities transfer to the basketball game through improved layups, dunks, rebounding, fast breaks, and defense.

WARMING UP

A proper warm-up is essential in preparing you for practice or competition. The warm-up increases muscle temperature, allowing for better stretching.

There are many options when it comes to warm-up activities. Some athletes warm up by jogging, jumping rope, doing calisthenics, doing a few agility drills from chapter 7, or by doing a dynamic warm-up.

A dynamic warm-up is the best way to prepare for basketball practice or play. It includes movements that are performed in the actual sport. A good dynamic warm-up for basketball features a variety of movements up and down the court, performed until you break a sweat. The following dynamic exercises are examples of a good basketball warm-up.

DYNAMIC WARM-UP EXERCISES

High Knee Skip

The High Knee Skip is a great warm-up exercise and it can also be used for developing speed. See page 162 in chapter 6, Speed.

Skip forward, driving your knee upward toward your chest with each skip. Use a full-range, exaggerated arm action; the opposite arm comes forward and up with each skip. The raised foot should be flexed upward (dorsiflexion).

High Knee Run

The High Knee Run is a great warm-up exercise and it can also be used for developing speed. See page 161 in chapter 6, Speed.

Move forward, using short, quick steps while raising your knees as high as your hips. The upper body remains upright; do not lean forward or backward. Use a shorter, quicker arm action than was used for the high knee skips.

Butt Kick

The Butt Kick is a great warm-up exercise and it can also be used for developing speed. See page 161 in chapter 6, Speed.

As you run forward, try to touch your gluteals with your heels. Thighs remain perpendicular to the floor. Lean your upper body slightly forward. Arm action is normal.

Carioca

Face sideways and move laterally by swiveling your hips and stepping so that your trail leg crosses in front of your lead leg. Then step to the side with your lead leg and cross behind with your trail leg. Continue this step-in-front, step-behind pattern with the trail leg. Make sure you carioca in both directions, to the right and left.

Lateral Shuffle

Face sideways as you move laterally by stepping with your lead foot and then bringing your trail foot up toward your lead foot without crossing your feet. Keep your body square; do not twist or rotate. Upper body leans forward slightly. Arms are in a slightly flexed ready position. Make sure you lateral shuffle in both directions, to the right and left.

Walking Lunge

Take a big step forward, lowering your hips and bending your knee until your lead thigh is parallel to the floor and your shin is straight up and down. Keep your trail leg as straight as possible, and your knee should not touch the floor. Step forward again, bringing your trail leg up to your lead leg, then continue with your trail leg as your lead leg. Keep your upper body upright and square.

Backward Run

Run backward while keeping your body square. Run with as big a stride as possible and maintain good arm action.

Side-to-Side Kick

Face a wall, standing 2 to 3 feet (.6 to .9 m) from the wall with your hands on the wall. Swing your right leg out to the side and back in front and across your body (figure 2.1). Continue this swinging pattern with your hips swiveling and your right leg slightly bent. Try to increase your range with each leg swing. Repeat with the left leg.

Figure 2.1

Front-and-Back Kick

Stand beside a wall with your left side closest to the wall and your left hand on the wall. Swing your slightly bent right leg forward and backward (figure 2.2). Continue this front-and-back swinging pattern, maintaining good posture. Do not arch or curl your back. Try to increase your range with each leg swing. Turn and repeat with the left leg.

Figure 2.2

Most dynamic warm-up activities combine several individual exercises. The following are some examples:

1. Do High Knee Skips down the length of the court and back.
2. Do High Knee Runs down the court and Butt Kicks back.
3. Carioca down the court with a 180-degree turn at half court so you move to both the right and left; lateral shuffle back with a 180-degree turn at half court.
4. Start with 4 Walking Lunges, then do Three-Quarter-Speed Strides to the end of the court; turn around and start with 4 Walking Lunges, then turn and Backward Run back.

After completing the movements up and down the court, face a wall and do 10 Side-to-Side Kicks with the right leg and 10 with the left leg. Then turn sideways and do 10 Front-and-Back Kicks with each leg. After the dynamic warm-up, you are ready to begin a stretching routine.

STRETCHING

Athletes often don't want to stretch. Sometimes that is because of bad previous experiences, a lack of understanding about the value of stretching, or the failure of coaches and trainers to offer them the best stretching programs for their needs. Several types of stretching programs exist; some are more practical and effective than others.

Static stretching consists of stretching a muscle in a fixed position for a given time; usually it's 15 to 30 seconds but it can be a minute or longer. Dynamic stretching involves controlled movements through a full range of motion. Often dynamic stretching is used as a transition phase between static stretching and practice or competition. In passive partner stretching, an athlete assumes a stretched position and has a partner assist by helping him or her reach a fuller stretching position.

Proprioceptive neuromuscular facilitation (PNF) stretching is an advanced form of stretching that also uses a partner. There are 2 main types of PNF stretching: the contract, hold, relax technique and the contract, move, relax technique. With the contract, hold, relax technique, the muscle is stretched to tightness and an isometric contraction is held for 5 to 10 seconds as the partner supplies resistance. The muscle then relaxes for 10 seconds and is then stretched farther before the next isometric contraction. This cycle is repeated 3 times. The contract, move, relax technique is similar, except during the contraction phase the joint is allowed to move at a predetermined range of motion.

One type of stretching that effectively warms the muscles, increases flexibility, and prepares athletes for practice and competition is active isolated stretching (AIS), developed by Aaron Mattes. AIS is different from conventional stretching in that the stretch is held for only 2 seconds at the full stretch position and 8 to 10 repetitions are performed. AIS is a great warm-up stretch because of the movement involved with each stretch. The movement also keeps athletes more focused during the stretch.

Follow these rules when performing active isolated stretching:

- Isolate the muscles being stretched.
- Inhale during the relaxed stage of the stretch and exhale when the stretch is being applied.
- Take the stretch as far as possible in a comfort zone.
- Hold each repetition for 2 seconds at the full stretch position and perform 8 to 10 repetitions of each stretch.
- Try to take the stretch a little farther with each repetition.
- Use proper technique and alignment with each stretch.
- Stretch daily.
- Stretch with a positive mental attitude and good focus.

Three routines can be performed, depending on preference and time available: the Full Stretch, the Basic Stretch, and the Quick Stretch. The Full Stretch involves each of the 20 stretches that follow, performed in the order in which they are presented. The Full Stretch should be done at least once a week. The Basic Stretch is the routine most often used and involves the upper-body and lower-body stretches (6 to 20) performed in the order in which they are presented. The Quick Stretch can be used if time is a factor. For the Quick Stretch, begin with the Lateral Trunk Stretch then perform all the lower-body stretches in order (11 to 20). The Quick Stretch should be done no more than twice a week.

These stretching routines are excellent as a team stretch before practices and games. They also should be used with individual workouts. After the stretch, you may want to continue to warm up with shooting or layup drills before doing more intense work.

The following AIS stretches follow a head-to-toe pattern, starting with the neck and finishing with the calves. The first 10 stretches are done from a standing position and the second 10 are done from a seated or lying position. Three of the stretches are done with a rope 8 to 10 feet long (2.4 to 3 m).

NECK STRETCHES

Since there are many stretches for the neck, do each neck stretch for only 5 repetitions instead of 8 to 10. You need to do neck stretches carefully with very controlled movements. Although the Neck Semicircles are not a true AIS stretch, they are a good warm-up for the rest of the neck stretches.

1. Neck Semicircle

Move your head in a semicircular motion (in the shape of a half moon). Start with your head in a neutral position, eyes straight ahead. Move your chin toward the top of your right shoulder, then lower it to your chest (figure 2.3) and continue in a semicircular movement toward the top of your left shoulder. Raise your head, returning to the neutral position, then move your chin back to your right shoulder. Continue this semicircular motion for the desired number of repetitions and then repeat the movement in the opposite direction, moving from left to right.

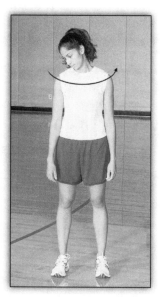

Figure 2.3

2. Chin to Chest

Tuck your chin to your chest (figure 2.4). Assist the end movement by carefully applying pressure on the back of your head with your hands. After each repetition, release the stretch and return to the neutral position.

Figure 2.4

3. Look-Up

Extend your head back as far as possible (figure 2.5). Assist the end movement by carefully applying pressure under your chin with your hands. Keep your mouth closed. After each repetition, release the stretch and return to the neutral position.

Figure 2.5

4. Ear to Shoulder

Move your head to the right with your right ear moving toward your right shoulder (figure 2.6). Assist the end movement by carefully applying pressure with your right hand, which is placed on the left side of your head from the top. After each repetition, release the stretch and return to the neutral position. Repeat the stretch to the left side.

Figure 2.6

5. Neck Rotation

Rotate your head to the right (figure 2.7). Assist the end movement by placing your right hand along the left side of your jaw and your left hand behind your head to the right and carefully apply pressure. After each repetition, release the stretch and return to the neutral position. Repeat the stretch to the left.

Figure 2.7

UPPER-BODY STRETCHES

The upper-body stretches are performed from a standing position. Although the Arm Circles are not a true AIS stretch, they are a good warm-up for the rest of the upper-body stretches.

6. Arm Circle

Stand with your arms straight out to your sides. Begin with small arm circles forward (figure 2.8), increasing the size of the arm circles with each repetition. After you complete the desired number of repetitions, reverse the movement, performing backward arm circles following the same pattern.

Figure 2.8

7. Pec Stretch

Stand with your arms straight out in front and your hands together, palms turned toward each other (figure 2.9a). Spread your arms out and back as far as possible while keeping your arms straight and parallel to the floor (figure 2.9b). After each repetition, return to the starting position with your palms together.

Figure 2.9

8. Lat Stretch

Stand with your arms at your sides and your palms facing forward (figure 2.10a). Keeping your right arm straight, raise it out to your side and up as high as possible. At the highest point, bring your right arm to the left behind your head (figure 2.10b). Assist the end movement by grasping your right elbow with your left hand from behind your head. Keep your right arm straight as you release the stretch, and return to the starting position after each repetition. Repeat the stretch with your left arm.

Figure 2.10

9. External and Internal Shoulder Rotation

Stand with your arms raised to your sides and parallel to the ground, elbows bent at a 90-degree angle, and hands forward with palms down (figure 2.11*a*). Rotate your shoulders and raise your forearms and hands up and back as far as possible (external rotation), keeping your elbows the same height as your shoulders (figure 2.11*b*). Return to the starting position.

After you finish the desired repetitions for external rotation, return to the starting position for internal rotation. Keeping your arms parallel to the ground, rotate your shoulders and lower your forearms and hands as far down and through as possible (figure 2.11*c*). Return to the starting position after each repetition.

Figure 2.11

10. Lateral Trunk Stretch

Stand with your arms overhead and grasp your elbows (figure 2.12a). Lean to the right as far as you can, assisting the stretch by pulling your left elbow with your right hand (figure 2.12b). Return to the starting position and repeat the stretch to your left. Continue this side-to-side movement for the desired number of repetitions.

Figure 2.12

LOWER-BODY STRETCHES

The lower-body stretches are performed from a seated or lying position. The stretches for the lower back are part of the lower-body stretches.

11. Knees to Chest

Lie on your back with your knees and hips flexed to 90 degrees and your feet off the floor (figure 2.13a). Bring your thighs toward your chest and place your hands just below your knees (figure 2.13b). Pull them toward your chest to assist the stretch. Release and return to the starting position after each repetition.

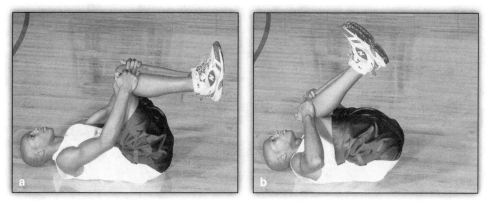

Figure 2.13

12. Leg Crossover

Lie on your back with your knees bent. Both feet are flat on the floor and close to your buttocks. Cross your right leg over your left leg and place your hands behind your head (figure 2.14a). Use your right leg to pull your left leg down to the right (figure 2.14b). Release and return to the starting position after each repetition. Repeat the stretch with your left leg over your right leg and pull to the left.

Figure 2.14

13. Glute Stretch

Lie on your back with your knees bent and both feet flat on the floor. Cross your right foot over your left knee (figure 2.15a). Raise your left foot off the floor and bring your left knee toward your chest. Assist the end movement by pulling your knee toward your chest, right hand at your right knee and left hand at your right ankle (figure 2.15b). Release the stretch and return the left foot to the floor after each repetition. Repeat the stretch with your left foot over your right knee.

Figure 2.15

14. Lower-Back Stretch

Sit on the floor with your legs wide apart and knees slightly bent (figure 2.16a). Tuck your chin to your chest and lean forward as far as possible. Assist the end movement by grabbing your heels and pulling forward a little farther (figure 2.16b). Release the stretch and return to the starting position after each repetition.

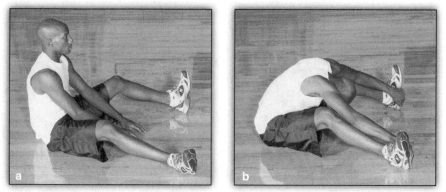

Figure 2.16

15. Bent-Knee Hamstring Stretch

You will need a rope for this stretch. Lie on your back with your left leg straight and on the floor. Your right knee is bent and raised above your right hip with your thigh perpendicular to the floor (figure 2.17a). Place the middle of a rope under the midline of your right foot and hold the ends of the rope in your left hand. Your right hand should be behind your right knee to help keep your thigh in the proper position. Straighten your right leg and assist the end movement by gently pulling on the rope (figure 2.17b). Release the stretch and return to the starting position after each repetition. Repeat with the left leg.

Figure 2.17

16. Straight-Leg Hamstring Stretch

You will need a rope for this stretch. Lie on your back with your legs straight and on the floor. Place the middle of the rope under the midline of your right foot and hold the ends of the rope in each hand (figure 2.18*a*). Raise your right leg as high as possible, keeping it straight. Assist the end movement by gently pulling on the rope (figure 2.18*b*). Return to the starting position after each repetition. Repeat with the left leg.

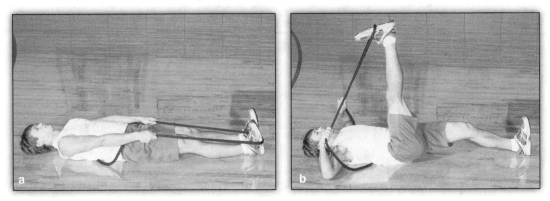

Figure 2.18

17. Seated Groin Stretch

Sit with your knees bent and the soles of your feet together (figure 2.19*a*). Spread your knees down toward the floor as much as possible. Assist the end movement by placing your hands, forearms, or elbows on the insides of your thighs and pressing down (figure 2.19*b*). Release the stretch and return to the starting position after each repetition.

Figure 2.19

18. Quad Stretch

Lie on your left side with both knees bent and raised toward your chest (figure 2.20a). Grab the top of your right foot with your right hand. Bring your right knee back and through toward your back as far as possible (figure 2.20b). Assist the end movement by pulling a little farther with your right hand. Return to the starting position after each repetition. Repeat with the left leg.

Figure 2.20

19. Straight-Leg Calf Stretch

You will need a rope for this stretch. Sit with your legs straight, together, and on the floor. Place the middle of a rope under the ball of your right foot and hold the ends of the rope in each hand (figure 2.21a). Point your right foot toward your right knee (figure 2.21b). Assist the end movement by gently pulling on the rope. Release and return to the starting position after each repetition. Repeat with the left leg.

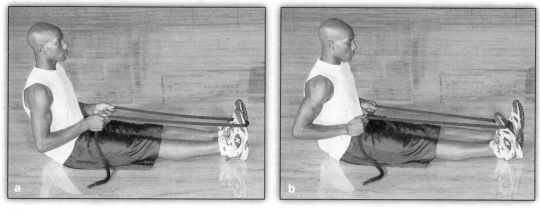

Figure 2.21

20. Bent-Knee Calf Stretch

Sit with your left leg straight and on the floor and your right leg bent (figure 2.22a). Move your right foot as close to your buttocks as possible. Raise your right foot toward your right knee, keeping your right heel on the floor (figure 2.22b). Assist the end movement by placing your hands under the ball of your right foot and pulling up. Release the stretch and return to the starting position after each repetition. Repeat with the left leg.

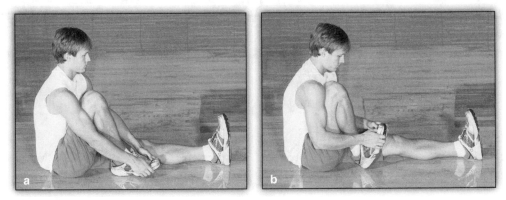

Figure 2.22

COOLING DOWN

Like a good warm-up, a postworkout cool-down is important. A cool-down enhances the recovery of the muscles and helps the body return to its resting state. A good cool-down includes low-intensity exercises such as easy jogging, shooting free throws, and stretching the major muscle groups—the lower back, glutes, quads, hamstrings, and groin.

Chapter 3

Conditioning

Playing basketball at a high level requires great conditioning. Being in great condition gives a player an advantage over an opponent and a team a better chance of winning. Players will be able to perform at maximum levels throughout the entire game. Lesser-conditioned athletes fatigue sooner, which negatively affects performance, resulting in slow defense and poor shooting and execution of plays. Look at this conditioning program as an opportunity to develop a better player.

Conditioning for basketball should be more than just playing basketball. For example, the off-season conditioning program should include 12 weeks of preparation, starting with 400s and 200s on a track and finishing with basketball-specific conditioning drills on the court.

ENERGY FOR PERFORMANCE

The body uses three separate energy systems: ATP-CP system, the glycogen lactic acid system, and the aerobic system. The ATP-CP and the glycogen lactic acid systems are anaerobic. The game of basketball is estimated to be 85 percent anaerobic and 15 percent aerobic. Therefore, most of the conditioning for basketball should be anaerobic in nature—repeated short, high-intensity efforts with quick recovery times.

Figure 3.1 shows that each energy system is based on time of exercise, and all systems work together during different time periods. The ATP-CP system is the energy source for approximately the first 10 seconds of high-intensity activity. Once the ATP-CP system is nearly depleted, more fuel for energy is available from the glycogen lactic acid system. This system lasts approximately 10 seconds to 2 minutes. The aerobic system slowly transitions in and is the main fuel source for longer, less intense activities.

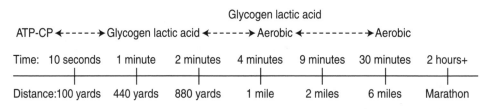

Figure 3.1 The primary energy systems, their exercise times, and approximate running distances. The arrows between the systems represent the transition phases from one system to another.

OPTIMAL RECOVERY FOR BASKETBALL

Basketball is a game of repeated, quick, high-intensity bursts of action with short rest periods in between. It is critical for players to be able to recover quickly during hard practices and games. Well-conditioned players recover more quickly and are able to maintain higher performance intensity for longer periods of time. By following the proper work–rest intervals in the 12-Week Off-Season Conditioning Program, you will develop and improve your recovery system.

Short-Term Recovery

A well-conditioned athlete can recover from intense bouts of work very fast. The ATP-CP energy system recovers 50 percent in about 30 seconds (the rest period during a free throw or 20-second timeout). It is fully recovered in 2 to 5 minutes (the rest time during timeouts, end of quarters, and when a player is taken out of the game). The glycogen lactic acid system recovers 50 percent in about 20 to 30 minutes and is fully recovered in 1 hour or more.

Long-Term Recovery

Long-term recovery can be from 2 days to several days depending on the extent of nutrient depletion, enzyme depletion, and tissue breakdown. A good diet that includes complex carbohydrates (the primary energy source for basketball), proper rest, and a quality training program will aid recovery, repair, and replenishment.

SEASONAL CONDITIONING PHASES

The 4 phases of seasonal conditioning are off-season, preseason, in-season, and postseason. Each phase has unique priorities. The off-season is the time to make the greatest gains in conditioning before the start of practices and games. The focus during the preseason and in-season phases is on practices and games. The postseason is the time for recovery.

Off-Season Conditioning

The 12-Week Off-Season Conditioning Program prepares you physically for the demands off a long, intense season. Find out when the first day of practice is, and start the conditioning program 12 weeks before that. The program starts with 400-meter strides on the track and progresses to basketball-specific conditioning on the court. Two conditioning workouts are scheduled per week and coincide with the two workouts per week of plyometrics and agility training in the off-season calendar. This is the progression of the 12-Week Off-Season Conditioning Program:

1. Two weeks of 400-meter strides
2. Two weeks of 200-meter strides
3. Two weeks of sprints
4. Two transition weeks (one day of sprints, one day of on-court conditioning)
5. Four weeks of on-court conditioning

If you play in a summer basketball league or play other sports, you may need to adjust the program to prevent possible overtraining. Signs of overtraining are a feeling of weakness in the weight room, not running as well on the track or court, or feeling fatigued. You can cut back on the complete conditioning program by doing just one day of conditioning and one day of plyometrics and agility drills each week or by doing fewer exercises each workout.

Preseason Conditioning

Preseason is the time between the first practice in the fall and the first game. This is the time when your coach fine-tunes conditioning with quality practices and the addition of more basketball-specific drills. Players who follow the off-season program will go into the preseason in great shape.

In-Season Conditioning

During the season, the majority of conditioning comes from practices and games. If practices include performing intense, all-out drills, running the court hard, and executing quality defensive work for 1 to 2 hours, you probably don't need extra conditioning. If you are not getting much playing time or need extra conditioning, choose from the on-court conditioning drills in the 12-Week Off-Season Program or use other shooting, passing, and dribbling drills. Off-court conditioning options include running on a treadmill, riding a stationary bike or elliptical trainer, using a stair climber, and swimming or running in a pool.

Postseason

The time immediately after the season and before the off-season is the postseason. Initially players should just recover physically from a long basketball season. Some athletes may go right into a spring sport such as baseball, tennis, or track. Some teams may have a postseason program that includes strength training, conditioning, and basketball skill development. For the others it is the "active rest" time of year.

During the active rest period, players should stay fit by playing other sports, by working out in the beginning phase of the strength training program, or by playing pickup basketball games. Players who are not getting any activity need to do some general fitness activities such as hiking, biking, jogging, or swimming. Conditioning on treadmills, stair climbers, elliptical trainers, or stationary bikes for 20 to 40 minutes, 2 or 3 times a week would also work.

ON-COURT CONDITIONING DRILLS FOR THE 12-WEEK OFF-SEASON CONDITIONING PROGRAM

The on-court conditioning drills are an essential transition phase from the track to the basketball-specific movements that are required when practices and games begin. The drills are designed for individual athletes and partners. They are not meant to be team drills.

Suicides

Start behind the baseline. Sprint to the near free-throw line and sprint back to the baseline (figure 3.2). Sprint to half court and sprint back to the baseline. Sprint to the far free-throw line and back to the baseline. Finish with a sprint to the far baseline and sprint back to the start. Sprint in a straight line.

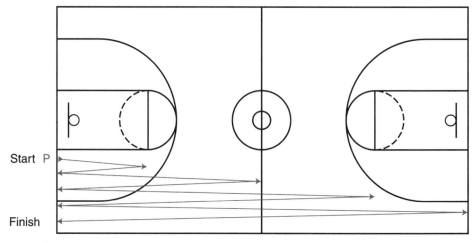

Figure 3.2

Deep 6s

Start behind the baseline and sprint to the far baseline. Turn around and sprint back to the start. Repeat this 3 times for a total of 6 lengths of the court (figure 3.3). Sprint in a straight line.

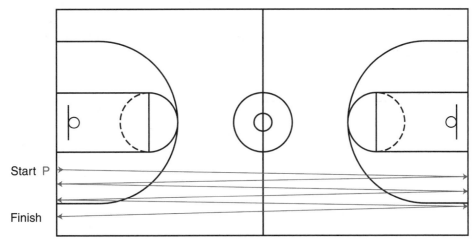

Figure 3.3

17s

Start behind a sideline and sprint to the other sideline and back (figure 3.4). Over and back is 2 repetitions; 1 repetition is 1 width of the court. Sprint in a straight line for a total of 17 repetitions.

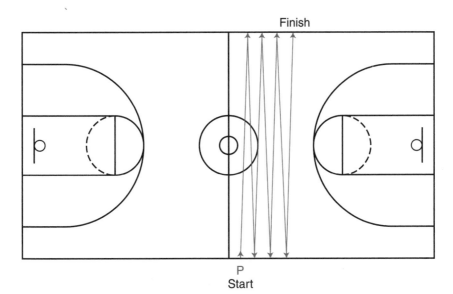

Figure 3.4

Accelerators

Accelerators feature 4 different speed transitions: jogging, striding, sprinting, and decelerating (slowing down).

Start behind the baseline. Jog to the near free-throw line, accelerate to a three-quarter speed stride to half court, then accelerate to a full-speed sprint to the far free-throw line (figure 3.5). Decelerate from the far free-throw line to the far baseline. Immediately turn around and repeat the 4 transitions for a total of 4 to 6 repetitions; 1 repetition is 1 length of the court.

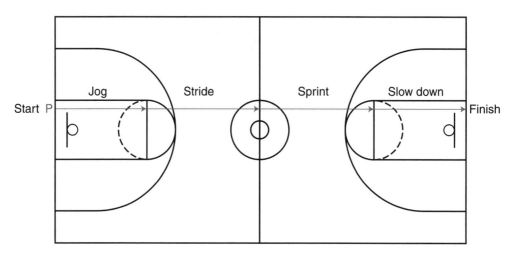

Figure 3.5

X Drill

The X Drill features a sprint and a defensive shuffle. Start in the lower right-hand corner facing the court. Sprint to the opposite corner and defensive shuffle to your right along the baseline to the corner (figure 3.6). Turn around and face the court. Sprint to the opposite corner and defensive shuffle to your left along the baseline back to the starting corner. Turn around and face the court. Repeat the sequence for 2 or 3 repetitions. (One repetition is 1 completed X on the court.)

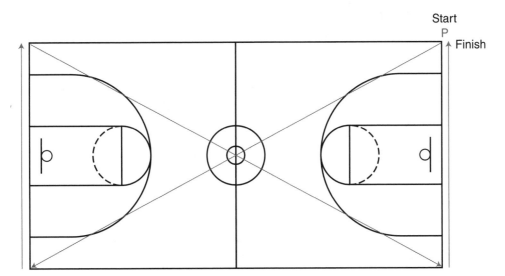

Figure 3.6

Ladder

The Ladder Drill consists of 4 sets of sprints with specific rest periods in between. Start behind a sideline. The first set of sprints is 15 repetitions from sideline to sideline, followed by a 1-minute rest period. The second set of sprints is 12 repetitions from sideline to sideline, followed by a 45-second rest period. The third set of sprints is 9 repetitions from sideline to sideline, followed by a 30-second rest period. The fourth set of sprints is 6 repetitions from sideline to sideline to complete the ladder. (One repetition is 1 width of the court. See figure 3.4 on page 43.)

DVD **Full-Court Sprint Dribble**

This sprint dribble conditioning drill uses both hands and full-court, half-court, and quarter-court dribbling hand exchanges.

Start behind the baseline, facing the court, holding a basketball. Sprint dribble with your right hand to the far baseline. Turn around and sprint dribble with your left hand back to the start (figure 3.7). Turn around and sprint dribble with your right hand to half court, then switch the dribble to your left hand and continue to the far baseline. Turn around and repeat the same sequence coming back. Turn around and sprint dribble with your right hand to the near free-throw line, then switch the dribble to your left hand and continue to half court. At half court, switch the dribble back to your right hand and continue to the far free-throw line. At the far free-throw line, switch the dribble back to your left hand and continue to the far baseline. Turn around and repeat the same sequence coming back. Dribble in a straight line using the outside edges of the free-throw lane. Six full lengths of the court completes the drill.

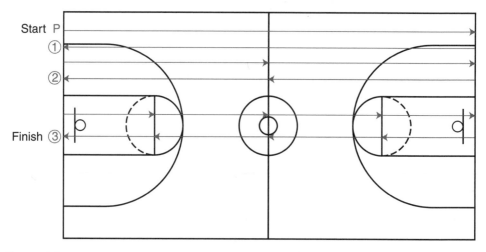

Figure 3.7

Advanced version: You may add a right-hand layup and left-hand layup at the appropriate ends.

Full-Court Zigzag Sprint Dribble

This sprint dribble conditioning drill uses both hands and changes of direction.

Start behind the baseline on the right outside edge of the free-throw lane, facing the court, holding a basketball. Sprint dribble with your left hand to the left corner of the free-throw lane (elbow) (figure 3.8). Switch the dribble to your right hand and continue to the right outside edge of the center jump circle. Switch the dribble back to your left hand and continue to the front left corner of the far free-throw lane (elbow). Switch the dribble back to your right hand and continue to the right baseline corner of the free-throw lane. Turn around and repeat the same sequence coming back, starting with a right-hand dribble. Repeat for a total of 4 to 6 repetitions. (One repetition is 1 length of the court.)

If you have cones available, you may set up your own zigzag patterns.

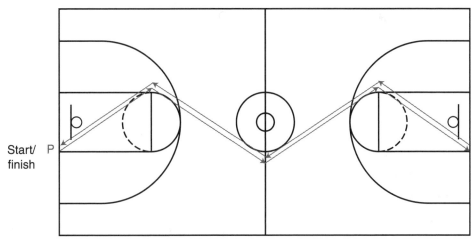

Figure 3.8

Advanced version: You may add a right-hand layup and left-hand layup at the appropriate ends.

DVD Full-Court Sprint With Chest Pass

This sprint conditioning drill uses chest passes and changes of direction. Two people and a basketball are needed for this drill.

Start with each partner standing behind the baseline at the outside edges of the free-throw lane, facing the court. One partner holds the basketball. Both partners start sprinting down the court, maintaining free-throw lane width, keeping their eyes on each other and the ball.

Perform quality two-hand chest passes back and forth between the partners (without traveling) to the far baseline. Touch the baseline and immediately turn around and return to the starting baseline, performing quality two-hand chest passes. Immediately turn around, face the court, and repeat the same sequence for a total of 4 to 6 repetitions. (One repetition is 1 length of the court.)

Variations: You can alter your passing-lane widths (farther apart or closer together). Also, the Full-Court Sprint With One Touch Pass is a variation shown on the DVD. In this drill, the passer uses two hands to catch but only one hand to throw.

Advanced version: Alternate layups between partners at each basket.

DVD Full-Court Sprint With Bounce Pass

This sprint conditioning drill uses bounce passes and changes of direction. Two people and a basketball are needed for this drill.

Start with each partner standing behind the baseline at the outside edges of the free-throw lane, facing the court. One partner holds the basketball. Both partners start sprinting down the court, maintaining free-throw lane width, keeping their eyes on each other and the ball.

Perform quality two-hand bounce passes back and forth between the partners (without traveling) to the far baseline. Touch the baseline and immediately turn around and return to the starting baseline, performing quality two-hand bounce passes. Immediately turn around, face the court, and repeat the same sequence for a total of 4 to 6 repetitions. (One repetition is 1 length of the court.)

Variation: You can alter your passing-lane widths (farther apart or closer together).

Advanced version: Alternate layups between partners at each basket.

Sideline Sprint Layup

This sprint layup conditioning drill uses both hands and changes of direction. Two people and a basketball are needed for this drill. One is the passer/rebounder and the other is the sprinter/shooter.

The sprinter/shooter starts behind the left sideline near the baseline, facing the basket. The passer/rebounder is in the lane near the basket with the ball, facing the shooter. The shooter sprints toward the basket while looking at the passer. The passer delivers a bounce pass in stride so that the shooter, without dribbling or traveling, is able to shoot a right-hand layup on the near side of the basket. The shooter continues without breaking stride, sprinting to the far sideline (figure 3.9). The passer rebounds the ball for the next pass. The shooter touches the sideline and immediately sprints back toward the basket as the passer delivers a bounce pass so the shooter can perform a left-hand layup on the near side of the basket without dribbling or traveling. The shooter continues to the far sideline without breaking stride. Repeat the same over-and-back sequence for a total of 3 to 5 repetitions. Sprint in a straight line without rounding the approach to the basket.

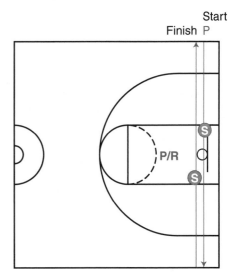

Figure 3.9

Variation: The Angled Sideline Sprint Layup is a variation shown on the DVD. In this drill, the sprinter/shooter starts at a 45-degree angle to the basket along the sideline.

Advanced versions: You may perform reverse layups on the far side of the basket or add 1 or 2 dribbles before each layup.

DVD **Half-Court Sprint, Elbow Jump Shot**

This sprint, jump shot conditioning drill features changes of direction. Two people and a basketball are needed for this drill. One is the passer/rebounder and the other is the sprinter/shooter.

The sprinter/shooter starts at half court in the center jump circle, facing the basket. The passer/rebounder is in the lane near the basket with the ball, facing the shooter. While looking at the passer, the shooter sprints toward the left elbow of the free-throw lane, slowing down under control before reaching the elbow (figure 3.10). The passer delivers a bounce pass in stride so that the shooter, without dribbling or traveling, is able to shoot a jump shot in rhythm from the elbow without floating toward the basket. After the shot, the shooter sprints back to the half-court starting point. The passer rebounds the ball for the next pass. The shooter touches half court and immediately sprints back toward the right elbow as the passer delivers a bounce pass to the shooter following the previously described techniques. Repeat the same left-elbow, right-elbow sequence for a total of 10 shots, 5 from each elbow.

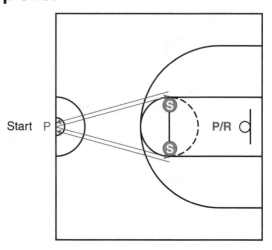

Figure 3.10

Advanced versions: The passer delivers the ball early so the shooter takes 1 or 2 dribbles before shooting. The shooter pump fakes a shot and takes 1 or 2 dribbles to the right or left before shooting.

12-WEEK OFF-SEASON CONDITIONING PROGRAM

Each off-season conditioning workout is shown in table 3.1. Note the different workouts, distances, repetitions, and rest intervals for each day. For example, on week 5, day 1, after warming up and stretching, stride 100 meters and rest 30 seconds. Stride 100 meters (or yards) back to the start and rest 30 seconds. Next stride 80 meters (or yards) and rest 30 seconds. Stride 80 meters (or yards) back to the start and rest 30 seconds. Then do 12 60-meter (or -yard) sprints down and back with a 30-second rest between each sprint. Finish the workout with a cool-down and stretch.

The 400-, 200-, 100-, and 80-meter (or yard) strides are good hard runs but not all-out efforts, about three-quarter speed. The sprints are all-out efforts and are 60 meters (or yards) and less. The on-court conditioning drills are also all-out efforts. You will get the best results by following the program closely.

Table 3.1 12-Week Off-Season Conditioning Program

Week	Day	Workout	Rest time
Week 1	Day 1	Stride 4 × 400*	2.5 min.
	Day 2	Stride 4 × 400	2.5 min.
Week 2	Day 1	Stride 6 × 400	2.5 min.
	Day 2	Stride 6 × 400	2 min.
Week 3	Day 1	Stride 10 × 200	1.5 min.
	Day 2	Stride 10 × 200	1.5 min.
Week 4	Day 1	Stride 12 × 200	1.5 min.
	Day 2	Stride 12 × 200	1 min.
Week 5	Day 1	Stride 2 × 100 Stride 2 × 80 Sprint 12 × 60	30 sec. 30 sec. 30 sec.
	Day 2	Stride 2 × 100 Stride 2 × 80 Sprint 12 × 40	30 sec. 30 sec. 30 sec.
Week 6	Day 1	Stride 2 × 100 Stride 2 × 80 Sprint 12 × 60	30 sec. 30 sec. 30 sec.
	Day 2	Stride 2 × 100 Stride 2 × 80 Sprint 12 × 40	30 sec. 30 sec. 30 sec.

(continued)

Table 3.1 *(continued)*

Week	Day	Workout	Rest time
Week 7	Day 1	Stride 2 × 100	30 sec.
		Stride 2 × 80	30 sec.
		Sprint 2 × 60	25 sec.
		Sprint 2 × 40	25 sec.
		Sprint 2 × 20	25 sec.
		Sprint 4 × 10	25 sec.
		Sprint 2 × 20	25 sec.
		Sprint 2 × 40	25 sec.
		Sprint 2 × 60	
	Day 2	Deep 6s × 2	25 sec.
		X Drill × 2	1 min.
		17s × 1	2 min.
Week 8	Day 1	Stride 2 × 100	30 sec.
		Stride 2 × 80	30 sec.
		Sprint 2 × 60	25 sec.
		Sprint 2 × 40	25 sec.
		Sprint 2 × 20	25 sec.
		Sprint 4 × 10	25 sec.
		Sprint 2 × 20	25 sec.
		Sprint 2 × 40	25 sec.
		Sprint 2 × 60	25 sec.
	Day 2	Suicides × 2	1 min.
		X Drill × 2	2 min.
		17s × 2	2 min.
Week 9	Day 1	Full-Court Sprint Dribble × 1	1 min.
		Full-Court Zigzag Sprint Dribble × 1	1 min.
		Sideline Sprint Layup × 2	1 min.
		X Drill × 2	2 min.
		Suicides × 2	1 min.
	Day 2	Full-Court Sprint With Chest Pass × 1	1 min.
		Full-Court Sprint With Bounce Pass × 1	1 min.
		Half-Court Sprint, Elbow Jump Shot × 2	1 min.
		Accelerators × 2	1 min.
		Ladder × 1	
Week 10	Day 1	Full-Court Sprint Dribble × 1	1 min.
		Full-Court Zigzag Sprint Dribble × 1	1 min.
		Sideline Sprint Layup × 2	1 min.
		X Drill × 2	2 min.
		Deep 6s × 2	1 min.
	Day 2	Full-Court Sprint With Chest Pass × 1	1 min.
		Full-Court Sprint With Bounce Pass × 1	1 min.
		Half-Court Sprint, Elbow Jump Shot × 2	1 min.
		Accelerators × 2	1 min.
		Ladder × 1	

Week	Day	Workout	Rest time
Week 11	Day 1	Full-Court Sprint Dribble × 1	1 min.
		Full-Court Zigzag Sprint Dribble × 1	1 min.
		Sideline Sprint Layup × 2	1 min.
		Full-Court Sprint With Chest Pass × 1	1 min.
		Full-Court Sprint With Bounce Pass × 1	1 min.
		Half-Court Sprint, Elbow Jump Shot × 2	1 min.
		X Drill × 1	2 min.
		17s × 1	
	Day 2	Full-Court Sprint Dribble × 1	1 min.
		Full-Court Zigzag Sprint Dribble × 1	1 min.
		Sideline Sprint Layup × 2	1 min.
		Full-Court Sprint With Chest Pass × 1	1 min.
		Full-Court Sprint With Bounce Pass × 1	1 min.
		Half-Court Sprint, Elbow Jump Shot × 2	1 min.
		Ladder × 1	
Week 12	Day 1	Full-Court Sprint Dribble × 1	1 min.
		Full-Court Zigzag Sprint Dribble × 1	1 min.
		Sideline Sprint Layup × 2	1 min.
		Full-Court Sprint With Chest Pass × 1	1 min.
		Full-Court Sprint With Bounce Pass × 1	1 min.
		Half-Court Sprint, Elbow Jump Shot × 2	1 min.
		X Drill × 1	2 min.
		17s × 1	
	Day 2	Full-Court Sprint Dribble × 1	1 min.
		Full-Court Zigzag Sprint Dribble × 1	1 min.
		Sideline Sprint Layup × 2	1 min.
		Full-Court Sprint With Chest Pass × 1	1 min.
		Full-Court Sprint With Bounce Pass × 1	1 min.
		Half-Court Sprint, Elbow Jump Shot × 2	1 min.
		Ladder × 1	

* Distances can be meters or yards, depending on the track or field being used.

Follow all track strides and sprints in the order listed for each workout. The on-court conditioning drills can be performed in the order listed, or all the drills for that workout can be performed one time through before the second repetition of each drill. When 17s or the Ladder Drill is listed, do those drills last.

CONDITIONING CIRCUITS ON THE BASKETBALL COURT

Conditioning circuits may replace an on-court conditioning day in the 12-Week Off-Season Conditioning Program. Individual, partner, or group circuits can be performed. A group circuit is defined as 2 or more circuit stations performed at the same time. Stations may use similar-themed exercises (for example, court running drills) or be mixed and varied with exercises from conditioning, speed, agility, and plyometrics with or without a basketball.

Conditioning circuit variables include the number of exercise stations, time of each station, time of each rest interval, work intensity of each station, and total circuit workout time. A proper warm-up and stretch are recommended before performing a conditioning circuit.

Caution: For safety reasons, with group or team circuits, make sure each station has enough space and does not interfere with other stations.

ON-COURT CONDITIONING DRILLS FOR INDIVIDUAL CIRCUITS

Suicides: See description on page 42.

Deep 6s: See description on page 43.

Sideline to Sideline: See following description.

Accelerators: See description on page 44.

X Drill: See description on page 45.

Full-Court Sprint Dribble: See description on page 46.

Full-Court Zigzag Sprint Dribble: See description on page 47.

Sideline to Sideline

Start behind a sideline. Sprint to the other sideline and sprint back to the start. Over and back is 2 repetitions; 1 repetition is 1 width of the court. Do as many as you can in 30 seconds. Sprint in a straight line. (See figure 3.4 on page 43.)

AGILITY DRILLS FOR INDIVIDUAL CIRCUITS

Lane Shuffle, Sprint, and Backpedal

This drill features shuffles, sprints, and backpedals and uses the free-throw lane.

Starting position: Start in a ready position behind the right corner of the baseline and lane, facing the court.

Action: Shuffle to your left across the lane and touch the line with your left foot. Immediately change directions and shuffle back to the start. Immediately sprint up the free-throw lane line to the free-throw line and shuffle to your left across the lane. Touch the line with your left foot and shuffle back. Quickly backpedal down the free-throw lane line to the starting position.

Caution: Be aware of the baseline wall during the backpedal finish.

Acceleration, Deceleration, Backpedal, Jump, and Shuffle

Setup: Set 4 cones 3 feet apart starting 3 feet from the left sideline along the free-throw line extended (3 feet, 6 feet, 9 feet, and 12 feet from the sideline, or about 1 meter, 2 meters, 3 meters, and 4 meters from the sideline).

Starting position: Start in a ready position behind the left corner of the baseline and sideline, facing the court.

Action: Sprint to the first cone and backpedal back to the baseline (figure 3.11). Sprint to the second cone and backpedal back to the baseline. Sprint to the third cone and backpedal back to the baseline. Sprint to the fourth cone and backpedal back to the baseline and the edge of the lane. Immediately jump as high as possible, then shuffle across the lane on the baseline and back.

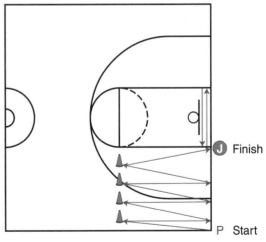

Caution: Do not step on the cones.

Figure 3.11

Backpedal, Hip Rotation, and Sprint

Setup: Set 3 cones in a staggered pattern on the free-throw lane lines extended between the free-throw lines.

Starting position: Start in a ready position behind the baseline in the middle of the free-throw lane, facing away from the court.

Action: Backpedal to the free-throw line (figure 3.12). Turn with good hip rotation and sprint around the 3 cones to the far free-throw line. Turn with good hip rotation and backpedal to the baseline.

Caution: Be aware of the baseline wall during the backpedal finish.

Advanced version: Vary the widths of the cones.

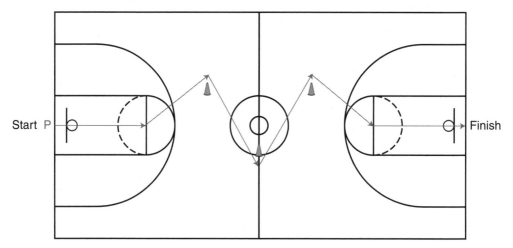

Figure 3.12

High-Speed Sprint Agility

Setup: Set 3 cones in a staggered pattern, 1 on the right sideline at half court and 2 on the center of each half court.

Starting position: Start in a ready position behind the right corner of the baseline and sideline, facing the court.

Action: Sprint around the 3 cones as fast as possible and finish at the far right baseline corner.

Lane Agility

This drill is the same as the lane agility test in chapter 1 (page 6). Set a cone in each of the 4 corners of the free-throw lane.

Starting position: Start in a ready position outside the left-hand corner of the free-throw line, facing the baseline.

Action: Sprint to the baseline past the cone. Defensive shuffle to the right past the cone, then backpedal to the free-throw line past the cone. Defensive shuffle to the left to the starting edge of the free-throw lane and touch the line with your left foot. Immediately change directions and defensive shuffle to the right past the cone. Sprint past the cone, defensive shuffle left past the cone, and backpedal back through the starting line.

Jump, Shuffle, Jump

The Jump Shuffle Jump Drill is done in the lane in front of the backboard.

Starting position: Start in a ready position in front of the right edge of the backboard, facing the baseline.

Action: Jump up as high as possible with both hands above your head and touch the backboard, if you are able. Land on both feet and immediately shuffle left and jump as high as possible, both hands above your head, in front of the left edge of the backboard. Shuffle back to the right edge of the backboard and jump as high as possible. Continue this over-and-back pattern for 3 to 5 repetitions. Over and back is 1 repetition.

Four-Way Closeout

This drill is done along the free-throw lane.

Starting position: Start in a ready position behind the baseline along the left side of the lane.

Action: Sprint up the lane to the free-throw line. Stop quickly in a defensive stance. Shuffle left at a 45-degree angle for 2 shuffles and right for 2 shuffles, then backpedal to the start (figure 3.13). Repeat on the other side of the lane.

Caution: Be aware of the baseline wall during the backpedal finish.

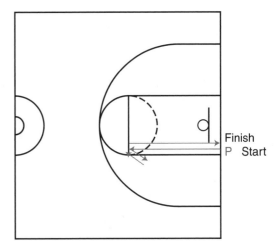

Figure 3.13

Five-Spot Closeout

Setup: Spread out 5 cones evenly around the three-point arc.

Starting position: Start in a ready position under the basket, facing the court.

Action: Sprint to cone 1, jump stop, and backpedal back to the start. Repeat to cones 2, 3, 4, and 5.

INDIVIDUAL ON-COURT CONDITIONING CIRCUITS

The individual circuits (table 3.2) may be performed as listed or used as examples of various possible court drill combinations.

Circuit stations and rest intervals are 30 seconds each. Use rest intervals to recover and prepare for the next exercise station. Complete the circuit once, in the proper exercise order (1 repetition of the circuit) before progressing to the second and third repetitions of the circuit in the same order.

Table 3.2 Sample Individual On-Court Conditioning Circuits

Four-station individual circuits			
Conditioning circuit		**Conditioning and agility circuit**	
1	Full-Court Sprint Dribble	1	Lane Agility
2	X Drill	2	Four-Way Closeout
3	Sideline to Sideline	3	Accelerators
4	Deep 6s	4	Full-Court Zigzag Sprint Dribble
Six-station individual circuits			
Agility circuit		**Conditioning and agility circuit**	
1	Lane Shuffle, Sprint, and Backpedal	1	Lane Agility
2	Acceleration, Deceleration, Backpedal, Jump, and Shuffle	2	Accelerators
3	Backpedal, Hip Rotation, and Sprint	3	Backpedal, Hip Rotation, and Sprint
4	High-Speed Sprint Agility	4	Suicides
5	Jump, Shuffle, Jump	5	Five-Spot Closeout
6	Five-Spot Closeout	6	Full-Court Sprint Dribble

ON-COURT CONDITIONING DRILLS FOR PARTNER CIRCUITS

Resistance Harness Running: See following description.

Double-Leg Power Dunk or Layup: See description on page 60.

Single-Leg Power Dunk or Layup: See description on page 60.

Jump, Shuffle, Jump With Two Basketballs: See description on page 60.

Partner Five-Spot Closeout: See description on page 61.

Full-Court Sprint With Chest and Bounce Passes: See description on page 61.

Sideline Sprint Layup: See description on page 49.

Half-Court Sprint, Elbow Jump Shot: See description on page 50.

Resistance Harness Running

This drill requires 2 people; partner 1 is the lead partner running against the resistance of partner 2, the trailing partner. Partner 1 wears the belt around the waist or the harness around the shoulders and waist. Partner 2 holds on to the handles at the end of the rope or tubing, which is attached to the belt or harness. The rope or tubing needs to be held tight without slack at the start and throughout the drill.

Starting position: Partner 1 stands behind the baseline, facing the court. Partner 1's feet are staggered and knees are slightly bent while leaning slightly forward at the waist. Elbows are flexed at a 90-degree angle and are at the sides. One hand is in front of the shoulder and the other hand is next to and slightly behind the hip. Partner 2 stands with the feet staggered and knees slightly bent while leaning slightly backward.

Action: Partner 1 drives the arms and knees forward and up in a powerful action while sprinting toward the far baseline for 30 seconds. Partner 2 controls the speed of the drill with the pace of his resistance trailing jog. After 30 seconds, partners switch positions and repeat the drill coming back.

Note: Run the full length of the court and start back if necessary.

DVD Double-Leg Power Dunk or Layup

Two people are needed for this drill: the shooter and rebounder/ball replacer. Place a basketball on each low block.

Starting position: The shooter stands under the basket, facing the court with his feet shoulder-width apart and his knees slightly bent. The rebounder/ball replacer is in the lane in front of and facing the basket.

Action: The shooter picks up a ball as fast as possible, then performs a drop step and jumps explosively as high as possible off of both legs for a dunk or layup. The shooter then immediately runs to the other ball and repeats. The shooter alternates from one block to the other block for 30 seconds. In between each shot, the rebounder/ball replacer immediately rebounds the ball and replaces it on the block. After 30 seconds, partners switch positions and repeat the drill.

Single-Leg Power Dunk or Layup

Two people are needed for this drill: a shooter and a passer/rebounder. The passer/rebounder is holding a basketball.

Starting position: The shooter stands on the right corner of the free-throw line and lane (the right elbow), facing the basket. The passer/rebounder is in the lane in front of the basket holding a ball and facing the shooter.

Action: The shooter starts toward the basket, receives a bounce pass from the passer, and, without dribbling jumps explosively as high as possible off of the left leg, dunking the ball or laying it up with the right hand. The shooter immediately runs to the left elbow as the passer rebounds the ball. The shooter turns and runs toward the basket to receive a bounce pass for a left-hand dunk or layup while jumping explosively off of the right leg. Continue this drill for 30 seconds. After 30 seconds, partners switch positions and repeat the drill.

Jump, Shuffle, Jump With Two Basketballs

Two people are needed for this drill: a shooter and a rebounder/ball replacer. The starting ball positions are on the floor under each corner of the backboard.

Starting position: The shooter starts in a ready position in front of the right edge of the backboard, facing the baseline and basketball. The rebounder/ball replacer is in the lane in front of and facing the basket.

Action: The shooter picks up the basketball and jumps explosively as high as possible off both legs for a dunk or layup. Landing on both feet, the shooter immediately shuffles left, picks up the basketball, and jumps explosively as high as possible off both legs for a dunk or layup. The shooter shuffles back to the right edge of the backboard, picks up the basketball, and jumps explosively as high as possible off both legs for a dunk or layup. Continue this over-and-back pattern for 30 seconds. In between each shot, the rebounder/ball replacer immediately rebounds the ball and replaces it. After 30 seconds, partners switch positions and repeat the drill.

Partner Five-Spot Closeout

Setup: Spread out 5 cones evenly around the three-point arc. (See figure 7.8 on page 182.)

Starting position: Partner 1 starts in a ready position under the basket. Partner 2 stands at cone 1 with a basketball, facing the basket.

Action: Partner 1 sprints to partner 2 and reacts to partner 2. If partner 2 pump fakes, partner 1 reacts to block the shot. If partner 2 moves to the right or left, partner 1 defensive shuffles a step or two to cut him off. Partner 1 backpedals back to the start as partner 2 moves to cone 2. Repeat to cones 2, 3, 4, and 5 or until 30 seconds are up. After 30 seconds, partners switch positions and repeat the drill.

Full-Court Sprint With Chest and Bounce Passes

This sprint conditioning drill uses chest passes, bounce passes, and changes of direction. Two people and a basketball are needed for this drill.

Start with each partner standing behind the baseline at the outside edges of the free-throw lane, facing the court. One partner holds the basketball. Both partners start sprinting down the court, maintaining free-throw lane width, keeping their eyes on each other and the ball. Perform quality two-hand chest passes back and forth between the partners (without traveling) to the far baseline. Touch the baseline and immediately turn around and return to the starting baseline, performing quality two-hand chest passes. Immediately turn around, face the court, and repeat the same sequence with bounce passes. Continue this alternating chest-pass, bounce-pass pattern for the full 30 seconds. After 30 seconds, partners switch positions and repeat the drill.

Variations: You can alter your passing-lane widths (farther apart or closer together).

Advanced version: Alternate layups between partners at each basket.

PARTNER ON-COURT CONDITIONING CIRCUITS

The sample partner circuits in table 3.3 may be performed as listed or used as examples of various possible court drill combinations.

Circuit stations and rest intervals are 30 seconds each. Partner 1 performs the exercise for the first 30 seconds; partner 2 performs the exercise for the second 30 seconds before rotating to the next exercise station. When doing partner circuits, immediately after exercising, switch positions and equipment if necessary. You may need an extra 5 to 10 seconds when switching exercise stations to change or set up equipment in the partner circuit. Complete the circuit once in the proper exercise order (1 repetition of the circuit) before progressing to the second and third repetitions of the circuit in the same order.

Table 3.3 Sample Partner On-Court Conditioning Circuits

Four-station partner circuit		Six-station partner circuit	
1	Jump, Shuffle, Jump With Two Basketballs	1	Resistance Harness Running
2	Single-Leg Power Dunk or Layup	2	Double-Leg Power Dunk or Layup
3	Full-Court Sprint With Chest and Bounce Passes	3	Partner Five-Spot Closeout
4	Sideline Sprint Layup	4	Half-Court Sprint, Elbow Jump Shot
		5	Full-Court Sprint With Chest and Bounce Passes
		6	Sideline Sprint Layup

Chapter 4

Strength

Many young athletes are motivated to work on the areas that will help them be more complete and better basketball players. The information in this chapter will show you how to increase performance by improving strength, power, speed, quickness, and flexibility. On the basketball court, that translates to jumping higher, shooting with greater range, and boxing out with more strength and power. Another area of improvement will be in confidence, as you see how newly increased levels in physical performance translate to the basketball court.

A common problem, however, is the vast amount of misinformation and improperly designed, unsafe, and inefficient strength training programs that are available. A properly designed, individualized, and functional strength training program for basketball increases performance and decreases the chances of injuries and their severity. This chapter contains safe and effective strength training programs with options for individuals for the different seasons of the year (off-season, preseason, in-season, and postseason).

The strength training programs emphasize strength and power development with the exception of the high-repetition programs, which emphasize muscular endurance. These programs are designed for healthy athletes and are not intended for physical therapy and rehabilitation. The information appears in the following sequence: fundamentals of strength training, core training (abdominals and lower back), core training techniques, strength training techniques, guidelines for sets and repetitions, and strength training programs. For safety reasons, we highly recommend you follow this order. Dedicated basketball players, coaches, and parents may all benefit from this information.

FUNDAMENTALS OF STRENGTH TRAINING

This section has important information that you will need in order to fully understand the strength training exercises and programs and how to use them properly and safely for the best results.

1. Proper and Safe Spacing   Before beginning any workout program, examine the workout area and plan ahead for whatever space you need in order to complete the workout in a safe and efficient manner. Look for unracked dumbbells or weight plates, loose collars, medicine balls, Swiss balls, or anything else on the floor that could cause an injury. Also check the flooring to make sure it is clean, dry, and not slippery.

When doing overhead exercises, make sure the ceiling is high enough so you can safely perform the exercise. Check for any low-hanging overhead lighting or anything hanging from the ceiling. Make sure there is enough room to perform the exercise without bumping into a wall, equipment, or other athletes. This is just common sense, but common sense goes a long way in preventing injuries.

2. Determining the Right Weight   Different methods can be used to determine the correct weight for an exercise. A popular method involves calculating certain percentages based on the maximum weight the athlete can lift for one repetition. We prefer using the trial-and-error method.

Start by warming up with a light weight to prevent injury and to prepare the muscles. Move up to a light comfortable weight for your first set. Then move the weight up each additional set until you have a weight that forces you to work very hard on the last 2 or 3 repetitions without compromising good technique for the prescribed sets and repetitions.

3. Lifting Belts   Many athletes choose to wear lifting belts while strength training. Belts should be used primarily for support and safety, not as a method of strengthening the back. Lifting belts help stabilize the muscles in the lower back and abdominals and are recommended for added support. Many athletes use lifting belts when attempting high-intensity overhead lifts such as the Push Press and Military Press. They are also used on the platform for exercises such as the Deadlift, Hang Clean, Snatch, and Squat.

When selecting a belt, choose one that is comfortable and provides the necessary support. Belts are available in different sizes, shapes, and materials.

When using a lifting belt, make sure that it fits snugly across the lower back and navel. Slightly loosen the belt between sets and tighten it when you begin your next set. Remember that the belt needs to be snug for support while you perform the exercise.

4. Breathing   Proper breathing technique is very important when strength training. The simple rule is to take a deep breath in and hold it during the beginning of the exercise, or the eccentric phase (lengthening of the muscle). Exhale during the finishing part of the movement, or the concentric phase (shortening of the muscle). For example, when doing the Bench Press, as your arms are extended straight up, take a deep breath and hold it while you bring the bar down to your chest, and exhale during the finishing part of the pressing movement. Repeat this process throughout each repetition. This method of breathing will allow for a large blood return to the heart, which reduces heart stress.

If you hold your breath throughout the exercise, cardiac problems such as elevated blood pressure and irregular heartbeats may occur. If you fail to breathe properly during weight training, you may experience the Valsalva effect. This reaction involves a rise in blood pressure, during which dizziness or fainting may occur.

For the explosive, Olympic-type movements, there are exceptions to these breathing rules. You hold your breath during the exertion phases of an Olympic-type movement and breathe in between the exertion phases.

5. Barbell Safety Checks Before you start lifting with a barbell, always check the following:

- Make sure you have the same weight on both sides of the bar.
- Be sure you have collars on both sides of the bar.
- Make sure the collars are secure.

6. Spotting Proper spotting is extremely important in any strength training program. Spotting involves observing or helping a person through an exercise. Helping involves assisting in raising the weight or aiding in the balancing of the weight when the lifter performs an exercise. When spotting, be sure to keep your eyes on the bar and the lifter at all times. Look for a breakdown in technique, a loss of balance, or a sticking point during the exercise.

Some exercises (such as Bench Press, Incline Bench Press, Seated Dumbbell Shoulder Press) may require a lift-off to start the movement. For a balanced lift-off, the spotter's hands should be evenly spaced on the bar with one hand over the bar and one hand under the bar. Here is a good procedure to follow:

1. The lifter or spotter counts to 3.
2. On the count of 3, the spotter and the lifter lift the bar to the starting position together.
3. Once the lifter has the bar under control, the spotter removes his hands from the bar and the lifter starts the exercise.
4. The spotter should also help the lifter rerack the weight at the completion of the exercise.

When spotting a lifter using dumbbells, watch to see if the dumbbells stray from the proper exercise groove. If they do, grab the lifter's wrists and help guide the dumbbells back into the proper groove.

7. Proper Range of Motion   To keep flexibility in the joints and muscles, train through the proper range of motion. If you do not train through the proper range of motion, there is a chance the muscles will shorten, causing a lack of flexibility and increasing your chance of injury. For example, during the Biceps Curl, the arms should hang straight down at the start and be fully flexed at the elbow joint at the top. Imagine the effect of shooting a basketball if the biceps had lost some flexibility and limited the range of motion during the follow-through. If you continually shorten the movement in this exercise, the biceps would begin to lose its range of motion and that could affect proper shooting technique. This may also lead to an injury.

8. Speed of Movement   The speed in which an exercise is performed is very important. If you perform a lift too fast, you are likely to perform it incorrectly, risking potential injury. Control both the lowering and the raising phases of the lift. Each repetition should be a smooth, controlled movement. An exception is the explosive Olympic movements. Perform those movements as fast as possible with proper technique.

9. Rest Between Sets   Rest periods between sets vary according to strength training goals. For example, low-intensity, high-volume workouts, such as circuit training with lighter weights, require less recovery time. The rest period between these sets can be 30 to 60 seconds. The goal is to increase muscular endurance and conditioning. High-intensity, low-volume training that uses sets and repetitions with heavy weight will require more rest and recovery time. The rest period between those sets can be 3 to 5 minutes. The goal is to increase strength and power. A good general guideline for recovery is 30 seconds to 2 minutes for lower-intensity, lighter-weight workouts and 3 to 5 minutes for higher-intensity, heavier-weight workouts.

10. Exercise Order   When planning a workout, outline a plan of attack for each training session. Target the major muscle groups first and then work the smaller muscle groups. When doing a lower-body workout, first perform Hang Cleans, Squats, Leg Press, Lunges, and Step-Ups. When doing a Total-Body Program in the same day, split the body in half and follow the exercise order for both upper-body and lower-body exercises. The exercises in the strength training programs are in the proper exercise order. An exception to this exercise order is in the Total-Body Circuit Program. With a group circuit, some athletes may have to start with small muscle groups first.

CORE TRAINING

Core training is a relatively new term used for working the muscles of the abdominals and lower back (the center of the body). The major muscle groups of the abdominals are transversus abdominis, internal obliques, external obliques, and rectus abdominis. The major muscle groups of the lower back are the erector spinae, which include spinalis, longissimus, and iliocostalis. There are other muscles included in the core; we identified the major muscles only. The core muscles enable you to flex, extend, rotate, and stabilize your torso and spine.

A strong and well-conditioned core helps maintain greater stability and proper body alignment as well as improve performance in many areas:

- It helps generate more power in several functional movements (such as running and jumping).
- It helps improve stamina and endurance.
- It helps reduce the chances of injuries and their severity.
- It helps develop a better and more complete basketball player.

We have developed core abdominal and lower-back exercise categories.

Core Abdominal Exercise Categories
- Trunk flexion (flexing spine, moving torso forward toward legs and hips)
- Hip flexion (flexing hips, moving legs toward torso)
- Rotary torso (rotating torso to the right and left)

Core Lower-Back Exercise Categories
- Trunk extension (extending torso backward toward legs and hips)
- Hip extension (extending hips, moving legs backward toward torso)
- Total-core stabilization (combination exercises that involve abdominals, lower back, and hips)

Core training may use various types of equipment for the exercises—back extension bench, glute/ham bench, flat bench, pull-up bar, medicine balls, Swiss balls, balance boards, disc, pads, rubber tubing, and bands.

The 34 core program exercises are identified as beginning, intermediate, and advanced within each category (table 4.1). Start with the beginning-level exercises. You must complete all beginning-level exercises with proper technique before progressing to the intermediate-level exercises. To progress to the advanced-level exercises, you must complete all the intermediate-level exercises with proper technique. As you progress in levels, you may still do exercises from the previous levels. Hundreds of core exercises are available. We have chosen beginning, intermediate, and advanced exercises within each of the six core categories. The exercise choices for each core category are listed on each workout card (see chapter 8). The sets and repetitions for the core exercises are also listed on each workout card.

Table 4.1   Core Exercises by Category

Abdominals			
	Beginning	**Intermediate**	**Advanced**

Trunk flexion	Crunch
	Quick Touch
		Full Sit-Up
		Weighted Crunch
			Medicine Ball Sit-Up
			  Toss
			Swiss Ball Crunch
			  With a Medicine
			  Ball

Hip flexion	Leg Raise Circle
	Leg Raise
		Leg Thrust
		Hanging Knee-Up
			Hanging Straight-
			  Leg Raise
			Hanging Knee-Up
			  With a Medicine
			  Ball

Rotary	Half Bicycle
	Twisting Sit-Up
		Hanging Diagonal
		  Raise
		Medicine Ball
		  Twisting Sit-Up
			Hanging Diagonal
			  Raise With a
			  Medicine Ball
			Three-Way Leg
			  Push-Down

Lower Back			
	Beginning	**Intermediate**	**Advanced**

Trunk extension	Swiss Ball Back
	  Extension
	Half Superman
	  Shoulder Raise
		Medicine Ball
		  Partner Over-Under
		Straight-Leg Deadlift
		  (Two Feet, One
		  Dumbbell)
			Straight Leg Deadlift
			  (One Foot, Two
			  Dumbbells)
			Straight Leg Deadlift
			  (One Foot, One
			  Dumbbell)

Hip extension	Swiss Ball Reverse
	  Hyperextension
	Superman
		Reverse
		  Hyperextension
		Alternating
		  Superman
			Weighted Reverse
			  Hyperextension
			Swiss Ball
			  Alternating
			  Superman

Total-core stabilization	Four-Way
	  Stabilization
		Medicine Ball
		  Partner Rotation
		Slideouts
			Four-Way
			  Stabilization With
			  Movement

CORE TRAINING TECHNIQUES

This section contains 34 core training exercises with photos and explanations. Each explanation shows the correct technique for the best results. To be on the safe side, have a qualified coach or instructor evaluate your technique.

TRUNK FLEXION

Crunch

1. Lie in the bent-knee sit-up position with your lower back flat against the floor, your forearms crossed over your chest, and your fingers touching your shoulders.
2. Tighten your abdominals and raise your shoulders and upper back about 30 to 45 degrees off the floor (figure 4.1).
3. Slowly return to the starting position. Keep your arms in place and relaxed throughout the exercise.

Figure 4.1

Quick Touch

1. Lie on the floor on your back with your arms and legs straight up.
2. Keeping your arms and legs straight up, reach up toward your toes quickly (figure 4.2). Don't completely return your back flat to the floor between repetitions.

Figure 4.2

Full Sit-Up

1. Lie in the standard bent-knee sit-up position with your lower back flat against the floor and your hands behind your head.
2. Tighten your abdominals and raise your torso to a straight up position (figure 4.3).
3. Slowly return to the starting position. Keep your arms in place and relaxed throughout the exercise.

Figure 4.3

Weighted Crunch

1. Lie in the standard bent-knee sit-up position with your lower back flat against the floor. With both hands, hold a weight plate or medicine ball to your chest.

2. Tighten your abdominals and raise your shoulders and upper back about 30 to 45 degrees off the floor (figure 4.4).

Figure 4.4

3. Slowly return to the starting position. Keep the weight on your chest throughout the exercise.

Medicine Ball Sit-Up Toss

1. Start in a seated position with your knees bent and your feet flat on the floor.

2. Have a partner stand 4 to 6 feet (about 1.2 to 2 m) in front of you, facing you and holding a medicine ball in both hands.

3. Your partner tosses the medicine ball to your hands in front of your chest.

4. Catch the ball and slowly descend to the floor. Return to the starting position.

5. At the starting position, pass the medicine ball back to your partner using a two-hand chest pass (figure 4.5).

Figure 4.5

Swiss Ball Crunch With a Medicine Ball

1. Lie on a Swiss ball with a flat back, bent knees, and feet flat on the floor.
2. Hold a medicine ball in both hands with straight arms directly over your face.
3. Tighten your abdominal muscles as you push your lower back into the Swiss ball while maintaining your balance.
4. Raise the medicine ball toward the ceiling while keeping your arms straight and perform a crunch (figure 4.6).
5. Slowly return to the starting position.

Figure 4.6

HIP FLEXION

Leg Raise Circle

1. Lie on your back. Place your hands palms down under your pelvis. Your hands and arms should function as a cradle to prevent your lower back from arching.
2. Keep your head and shoulders up with abdominals flexed to flatten your lower back against the floor. This limits the strain on the lower back.
3. Raise your legs 6 inches (15 cm) off the floor (figure 4.7). Perform 12-inch (30 cm) small circles both clockwise and counterclockwise for an equal number of repetitions.

Figure 4.7

Leg Raise

1. Lie on your back. Place your hands palms down under your pelvis. Your hands and arms function as a cradle to prevent your lower back from arching.
2. Keep your head and shoulders up with abdominals flexed to flatten your lower back against the floor. This limits the strain on the lower back.
3. Raise your legs 12 inches (30 cm) off the floor, then up to 18 inches (45 cm), then back down to 12 inches (figure 4.8).

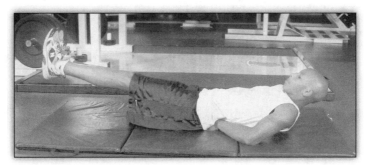

Figure 4.8

 ## Leg Thrust

1. Lie on your back. Place your hands palms down under your pelvis. Your hands and arms function as a cradle to prevent your lower back from arching.
2. Keep your head and shoulders up with abdominals flexed to flatten your lower back against the floor. This limits the strain on the lower back.
3. Raise your legs 6 inches (15 cm) off the floor. Bring your knees toward your chest then extend your legs straight up, raising your hips 6 inches off the floor (figure 4.9).
4. Lower your hips to the floor and return your legs to 6 inches off the floor by reversing the technique.

Figure 4.9

Hanging Knee-Up

DVD

1. For this exercise, you will need a chin-up bar. On the chin-up bar, take a slightly wider than shoulder-width grip with straight arms. Keep your upper torso relaxed with your legs hanging straight down.

2. Raise your knees to your chest (figure 4.10) then lower your legs back down under control until they are hanging straight.

3. The more you curl your spine at the top of the movement, the greater the abdominal involvement.

Figure 4.10

Hanging Straight-Leg Raise

DVD

1. For this exercise, you will need a chin-up bar. On the chin-up bar, take a slightly wider than shoulder-width grip with straight arms. Keep your upper torso relaxed with your legs hanging straight down.

2. Tighten your abdominal muscles. Raise your legs as high as possible while keeping them straight (figure 4.11). Then lower your legs under control until they are hanging straight.

Figure 4.11

Hanging Knee-Up With a Medicine Ball

1. On a chin-up bar, take a slightly wider than shoulder-width grip with straight arms. Keep your upper torso relaxed with your legs hanging straight down. Hold a medicine ball between your knees.

2. Raise your knees to your chest (figure 4.12) then lower your legs under control until they are hanging straight.

3. The more you curl your spine at the top of the movement, the greater the abdominal involvement.

Figure 4.12

ROTARY

 ## Half Bicycle

1. Lie on your back with a 90-degree angle at both hips and knees and your hands behind your head.

2. Tighten your abdominal muscles. In a cycling motion, move your right elbow and left knee toward each other and touch quickly (figure 4.13).

3. Repeat with your left elbow and right knee.

Figure 4.13

Twisting Sit-Up

1. Lie in the standard bent-knee sit-up position with your lower back flat against the floor and your hands behind your head.

2. Tighten your abdominals and raise your torso up as you twist, touching your right elbow to your left knee (figure 4.14).

3. Slowly return to the starting position. Repeat with your left elbow touching your right knee.

Figure 4.14

Hanging Diagonal Raise

1. On a chin-up bar, take a slightly wider than shoulder-width grip with straight arms. Keep your upper torso relaxed with your legs hanging straight down.

2. Raise your knees diagonally to the right as high as possible (figure 4.15) then lower your legs under control until they are hanging straight.

3. Repeat the diagonal movement to the left.

4. The more you curl your spine at the top of the movement, the greater the abdominal involvement.

Figure 4.15

Medicine Ball Twisting Sit-Up

1. Lie in the standard bent-knee sit-up position with your lower back flat against the floor. Hold a medicine ball on your chest with both hands.

2. Tighten your abdominals and raise your shoulders and upper back about 45 to 60 degrees off the floor. Rotate your torso to the left and touch the medicine ball to the floor next to your left hip (figure 4.16).

3. Slowly return to the starting position and repeat the same movement, rotating to the right.

Figure 4.16

Advanced version:

The Medicine Ball Touch, a more advanced variation of Medicine Ball Twisting Sit-Ups, can be viewed on the DVD.

Hanging Diagonal Raise With a Medicine Ball

1. On a chin-up bar, take a slightly wider than shoulder-width grip with straight arms. Keep your upper torso relaxed with your legs hanging straight down. Hold a medicine ball between your knees.

2. Raise your knees diagonally to the right as high as possible then lower your legs under control until they are hanging straight.

3. Repeat the diagonal movement to the left (figure 4.17).

4. The more you curl your spine at the top of the movement, the greater the abdominal involvement.

Figure 4.17

Three-Way Leg Push-Down

1. Lie on the floor on your back with legs straight up.
2. Your partner stands facing you with his feet on each side of your head.
3. Your arms are bent and your hands are holding your partner's ankles for stability (figure 4.18a).
4. Your partner pushes both of your legs straight down toward the floor (figure 4.18b).
5. Resist and stop the downward movement as quickly as possible without your feet touching the floor. Then with straight legs, quickly return to the starting position.
6. Your partner then repeats the push-down to the right, to the left, and back to the middle to start the same three-way sequence again.

Figure 4.18

TRUNK EXTENSION

DVD Swiss Ball Back Extension

1. Lie facedown on a Swiss ball with your abdominals on top of the ball, your head and shoulders facing the floor, and your feet stabilized, either fixed or held.
2. Raise your torso until your body is straight and fully extended (figure 4.19). Lower back down under control.

Figure 4.19

Half Superman Shoulder Raise

1. Lie facedown on the floor with your arms reaching straight out in front of you and your legs straight.
2. Keeping your arms straight, reaching out in front of you, raise your shoulders 2 to 6 inches (5 to 15 cm) off the floor and hold for 2 to 10 seconds (figure 4.20). Lower back to the floor under control.

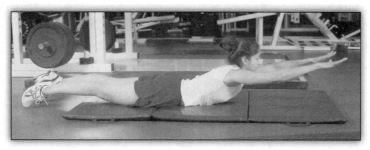

Figure 4.20

Medicine Ball Partner Over–Under

1. Stand back to back with a partner, approximately 2 feet (.6 m) apart, feet slightly wider than hip-width apart.
2. Both of you should hold your arms straight down in front.
3. Hold a medicine ball with both hands on the sides of the ball.
4. Raise the medicine ball overhead with straight arms. Your partner raises his arms overhead with his hands offset from your hands to receive the ball (figure 4.21a).
5. Immediately both of you bend over as your partner hands off the ball between his legs to you. Receive the ball by reaching between your legs (figure 4.21b).
6. Hand off and receive the ball at the midline extended between you and your partner.
7. Repeat for equal repetitions in the opposite direction.

Figure 4.21

Straight-Leg Deadlift (Two Feet, One Dumbbell)

1. Stand with feet hip-width apart.
2. Hold a dumbbell in your right hand, arm straight, with your right hand in front of your right thigh (figure 4.22a). Your left arm is straight and at your side.
3. With legs straight or slightly bent, slowly bend over with a straight back, lowering the dumbbell in front of your legs diagonally to the top of your left foot (figure 4.22b). Do not round your back.
4. Slowly return with a straight back to a full standing position. Do not bang the dumbbell on the floor or bounce at the bottom.

Figure 4.22

 ## Straight-Leg Deadlift (One Foot, Two Dumbbells)

1. Stand with feet hip-width apart and your right foot just off the floor.
2. Hold a dumbbell in each hand, arms straight.
3. With your left leg straight or slightly bent, slowly bend over with a straight back, lowering the dumbbells straight down in front of your legs. Your right leg goes straight back behind you until it is parallel to the floor (figure 4.23). Do not round your back; keep your hips square.
4. Slowly return with a straight back to a full standing position. Do not bang the dumbbells on the floor or bounce at the bottom.
5. Repeat while balanced on your right foot.

Figure 4.23

Straight-Leg Deadlift (One Foot, One Dumbbell)

1. Stand with feet hip-width apart and your right foot just off the floor.
2. Hold a dumbbell in your right hand, arm straight, with your right hand in front of your right thigh. Your left arm is straight and at your side.
3. With legs straight or slightly bent, slowly bend over with a straight back, lowering the dumbbell in front of your legs diagonally to the top of your left foot without moving your right leg (figure 4.24). Do not round your back.
4. Slowly return with a straight back to a full standing position. Do not bang the dumbbell on the floor or bounce at the bottom.
5. Repeat while balanced on your right foot.

Figure 4.24

HIP EXTENSION

Swiss Ball Reverse Hyperextension

1. Lie facedown on a Swiss ball with your abdominals on top of the ball and your legs straight, toes touching the floor.
2. Your head and shoulders face the floor. Touch the floor with your forearms or hands for stability.
3. Raise your legs, keeping them straight, until your body is straight and fully extended (figure 4.25). Lower back down under control until your toes touch the floor.

Figure 4.25

Superman

1. Lie facedown on the floor with your arms reaching straight out in front of you and your legs straight.

2. Keeping your arms straight, reaching out in front of you, raise your shoulders and feet 2 to 6 inches (5 to 15 cm) off the floor and hold for 2 to 10 seconds (figure 4.26). Lower back to the floor under control.

3. In the up position, keep your body as straight and long as possible.

Figure 4.26

 ## Reverse Hyperextension

1. Lie facedown on a high bench or reverse hyperextension machine and hold on with your hands.

2. Your legs hang straight down toward the floor.

3. Raise your legs, keeping them straight, until your body is straight and fully extended (figure 4.27). Lower your legs back down under control to the starting position.

Figure 4.27

Alternating Superman

1. Lie facedown on the floor with your arms reaching straight out in front of you and your legs straight.
2. Raise your right leg and left arm 2 to 6 inches (5 to 15 cm) off the floor at the same time (figure 4.28). Hold for 2 to 10 seconds under control.
3. Repeat with the left leg and right arm.
4. In the up position, keep your body as straight and long as possible.

Figure 4.28

Weighted Reverse Hyperextension

1. Lie facedown on a high bench or reverse hyperextension machine and hold on with your hands.

2. Your legs hang straight down toward the floor. If you are using a high bench, wear ankle weights. If you are using a reverse hyperextension machine, the pad should be slightly above your heels.

3. Raise your legs, keeping them straight, until your body is straight and fully extended (figure 4.29). Lower your legs back down under control to the starting position.

Figure 4.29

Swiss Ball Alternating Superman

1. Lie facedown on a Swiss ball with your abdominals on top of the ball, your head and shoulders facing the floor, and your toes touching the floor.

2. Raise your right leg and left arm 2 to 6 inches (5 to 15 cm) above your torso at the same time. Hold for 2 to 10 seconds under control.

3. Repeat with your left leg and right arm (figure 4.30).

4. In the up position, keep your body as straight and long as possible.

Figure 4.30

5. Caution: Maintaining balance and proper position is important for safety.

TOTAL-CORE STABILIZATION

Four-Way Stabilization

Prone Position

1. Lie facedown on the floor with your body straight and your arms out in front of you.

2. Raise your upper body and bring your elbows under your shoulders with your forearms on the floor and angled in. Your hands can be in fists or palms down on the floor.

3. Raise your body up off the floor, keeping it straight and tight (figure 4.31a). Your forearms, hands, and toes are touching the floor.

4. Hold this straight position for 30 to 60 seconds. Do not let your body sag down or your butt rise up.

Figure 4.31　Prone position

Supine Position

1. Lie on your back on the floor with your body straight and your arms at your sides.

2. Raise your upper body and bring your elbows under your shoulders with your forearms next to your body. Your hands can be in fists or palms down on the floor.

3. Raise your body up off the floor, keeping it straight and tight (figure 4.31*b*). Your forearms, hands, and heels are touching the floor.

4. Hold this straight position for 30 to 60 seconds. Do not let your body sag down.

Figure 4.31   Supine position

Side Position

1. Lie on your left side on the floor with your body straight and your left arm straight out in front of you. Your right arm can be on your right side or bent with your hand on your waist.

2. Raise your upper body and bring your left elbow under your shoulder with your forearm on the floor straight out in front of you. Your left hand can be a fist or palm down on the floor.

3. Raise your body up off the floor, keeping it straight and tight (figure 4.31*c*). Your forearm, hand, and outside of your left foot are touching the floor.

4. Hold this straight position for 30 to 60 seconds. Do not let your body sag down. Repeat this sequence on your right side.

Figure 4.31   Side position

Medicine Ball Partner Rotation

1. Stand back to back with a partner, approximately 2 feet (.6 m) apart.

2. Both of you should hold your arms at your sides, elbows flexed at about 90 degrees, forearms parallel to the floor.

3. Hold a medicine ball with your left hand on the upper-left side of the ball and your right hand on the lower-left side.

Figure 4.32

4. Rotate to the right to hand the medicine ball to your partner as your partner rotates to the left to receive the ball with his right hand on the upper-right side of the ball and his left hand on the lower-right side (figure 4.32a).

5. Immediately rotate to the left to receive the ball back from your partner, who rotates to the right to hand off the ball (figure 4.32b).

6. Hand off and receive the ball at the midline extended between you and your partner.

7. Repeat for equal repetitions in the opposite direction.

8. Perform the repetitions as quickly as possible. Be careful; you may become dizzy during the exercise.

Slideouts

1. Slideouts can be performed on a slide board or basketball floor.
2. Begin with your knees on a towel or padding on the floor.
3. Your arms are straight and hands are on a towel in front of your knees (figure 4.33*a*).
4. Keep your arms straight and your back and abdominals tight throughout the movement. Slide the towel out in front of you under control as far as you can with proper technique (figure 4.33*b*).
5. Return to the starting position.
6. Limit your reach if your back sags or you feel pain.

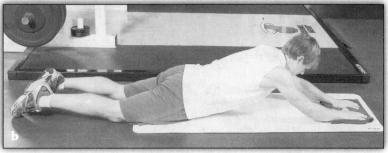

Figure 4.33

DVD Four-Way Stabilization With Movement

Prone Position

1. Lie facedown on the floor with your body straight and your arms out in front of you.

2. Raise your upper body and bring your elbows under your shoulders with your forearms on the floor and angled in. Your hands can be in fists or palms down on the floor.

3. Raise your body up off the floor, keeping it straight and tight (figure 4.34*a*). Your forearms, hands, and toes are touching the floor.

4. Raise your left leg as high as possible, keeping it straight while maintaining square and level hips (figure 4.34*b*). Then lower your left leg under control back to the starting position of the movement.

5. Raise your right leg as high as possible, keeping it straight while maintaining square and level hips. Then lower your right leg under control back to the starting position of the movement.

6. Continue this sequence for 10 repetitions.

Figure 4.34   Prone position

Supine Position

1. Lie on your back on the floor with your body straight and your arms at your sides.

2. Raise your upper body and bring your elbows under your shoulders with your forearms next to your body. Your hands can be in fists or palms down on the floor.

3. Raise your body up off the floor, keeping it straight and tight (figure 4.34c). Your forearms, hands, and heels are touching the floor.

4. Raise your right leg as high as possible, keeping it straight while maintaining square and level hips (figure 4.34d). Then lower your right leg under control back to the starting position of the movement.

5. Raise your left leg as high as possible, keeping it straight while maintaining square and level hips. Then lower your left leg under control back to the starting position of the movement.

6. Continue this sequence for 10 repetitions.

Figure 4.34   Supine position

Side Position

1. Lie on your left side on the floor with your body straight and your left arm straight out in front of you. Your right arm can be on your right side or bent with your hand on your waist.

2. Raise your upper body and bring your left elbow under your shoulder with your forearm on the floor straight out in front of you. Your left hand can be a fist or palm down on the floor.

3. Raise your body up off the floor, keeping it straight and tight (figure 4.34e). Your forearm, hand, and outside of your left foot are touching the floor.

4. Raise your right leg as high as possible, keeping it straight while maintaining a straight and tight body (figure 4.34f). Then lower your right leg under control back to the starting position of the movement.

5. Continue this movement for 5 to 10 repetitions. Then repeat on your right side, raising your left leg. Do not let your hips rotate when lifting your leg.

Figure 4.34   Side position

STRENGTH TRAINING TECHNIQUES

This section includes 45 strength training exercises, with photos and explanations for each exercise. Each explanation shows the correct technique for the best results.

Some words of caution: No two people are exactly alike. You need to be aware of individual differences as they relate to the proper technique in strength training exercises. First you should adjust the equipment and weight to fit your body and individual needs for each exercise. Very few people are capable of perfect technique on all lifts. Technique may vary depending on individual differences. You might have to make adjustments in range of motion, grips, stances, and grooves. To be on the safe side, have a qualified coach or instructor evaluate your lifting technique.

Squat

DVD

1. Place the bar on the rack just under the height of your shoulders so that you have to squat slightly to place the bar on the back of your shoulders.

2. Grip the barbell, hands in a medium to wide overhand grip. Raise your elbows to create a muscular shelf for the bar across the posterior deltoids and upper trapezius. Do not put the bar on your neck; it should be below your neck.

3. Stand with both feet and hips under the bar then straighten your legs to lift the bar off the rack.

4. Step back from the rack and get in a set position. Stand with feet slightly wider than the hips and toes pointed out slightly (figure 4.35a).

5. Keep your eyes, head, shoulders, and chest up and maintain a tight back throughout the lift.

Figure 4.35

6. Squat down under control, leading with your hips, until your thighs are parallel to the ground (figure 4.35b). Do not bounce at the bottom of the movement. Keep your knees in line with your toes; don't allow your knees to move inside or outside the normal tracking of the knee joint or move out in front of your toes. Keep your weight evenly distributed over your feet; do not shift your weight forward to your toes.

7. Raise the bar by straightening your hips and knees while maintaining correct body position. Keep your hips underneath you; do not round your back or lean forward on your feet.

Figure 4.35

8. When you have finished the set, slowly walk back into the rack with both feet and hips underneath the bar. Squat down and lower the bar onto the rack.

Spotting: Spot from behind, helping the lifter out of the rack. Squat each repetition with the lifter, hands underneath the bar or underneath the lifter's arms near the lifter's chest. Assist only if necessary by grabbing the bar or chest from underneath and both of you squat the weight up to a safe position. Walk forward and help the lifter safely into the rack. Hold the bar in and tell the lifter he or she can lower the bar. Adjust the safety bars inside the rack to just below parallel to catch the bar if needed.

DVD Hang Pull

1. Stand with your feet hip-width apart, bar near your shins.

2. Grip the bar in a closed pronated wide grip, palms turned toward your body.

3. Slowly stand up with the bar, keeping it close to your body. Keep your head and shoulders up. Use your legs to lift the weight. Maintain a tight, flat back and straight arms.

4. Cock the bar and slide it down your thighs to the power pulling position, just above your knees (figure 4.36).

5. Initiate the pull by explosively extending your legs, hips, and back, keeping your arms straight. Thrust your shoulders back and up. Thrust your hips forward and up.

Figure 4.36   Starting position for Hang Pull and Hang Clean

6. Straighten your legs and extend up onto your toes before your arms begin pulling. Keep the bar close to your body.

7. As the bar reaches your upper chest, slightly bend your knees to prevent back strain.

8. Slowly lower the bar, keeping it close to your body. To prevent lower back strain, as the bar descends it should brush your thighs and your knees should be slightly bent. Stand straight up then lower the bar to thigh level just above your knees and perform the next repetition. When you have performed all repetitions, slowly lower the weight to the floor, reversing the technique in step 3.

Hang Clean

1. Stand with your feet hip-width apart, bar near your shins.

2. Grip the bar in a closed pronated shoulder-width grip, palms turned toward your body.

3. Slowly stand up with the bar, keeping it close to your body. Keep your head and shoulders up. Use your legs to lift the weight. Maintain a tight, flat back and straight arms.

4. Cock the bar and slide it down your thighs to the power pulling position, just above your knees (figure 4.36).

5. Initiate the pull by explosively extending your legs, hips, and back, keeping your arms straight. Thrust your shoulders back and up. Thrust your hips forward and up.

6. Straighten your legs and extend up onto your toes before your arms begin pulling. Keep the bar close to your body.

7. As the bar reaches your upper chest, lower your body to a one-eighth to one-quarter squat position before the bar starts to descend in preparation for the catching or racking of the bar on your shoulders. Rotate your wrists back around and under the bar, lifting your elbows high out in front of the bar. Carry the bar on your shoulders with your knees slightly bent to cushion the impact. Stand up straight with the bar racked.

8. Slowly lower the bar, keeping it close to your body. To prevent lower back strain, as the bar descends it should brush your thighs and your knees should be slightly bent. Stand straight up then lower the bar to thigh level just above your knees and perform the next repetition. When you have performed all repetitions, slowly lower the weight to the floor, reversing the technique of step 3.

Power Clean and High Pull From the Ground

Start

1. Stand with your feet hip-width apart, bar near your shins.

2. Grip the bar with a closed pronated grip, palms turned toward your body, hands shoulder-width apart for a power clean and in a wide grip for a high pull. Keep your back tight and flat and your shoulders over the bar as you bend your knees and lower your hips to prepare for the first pull (figure 4.37a).

3. First pull: Slowly lift the bar from the floor, using your legs, keeping your shoulders over the bar and your back

Figure 4.37 Starting position and action

flat. Don't jerk the bar from the floor. Keep the bar close to your body and your butt down until the bar clears your knees. Lift your butt a little to prepare for the scoop (the second pulling phase of the lift).

4. Second pull: Initiate the second pull by explosively extending your legs, hips, and back, keeping your arms straight. Thrust your shoulders back and up. Thrust your hips forward and up.

5. Straighten your legs and extend up onto your toes before your arms begin pulling (figure 4.37b). Keep the bar close to your body.

Power Clean Finish

6. As the bar reaches your upper chest, lower your body to a one-eighth to one-quarter squat position before the bar starts to descend in preparation for the catching or racking of the bar on your shoulders. Rotate your wrists back around and under the bar, lifting your elbows high out in front of the bar. Carry the bar on your shoulders with your knees slightly bent to cushion the impact (figure 4.37c). Stand up straight with the bar racked.

7. Slowly lower the bar, keeping it close to your body. To prevent lower back strain, as the bar descends it should brush your thighs and your knees should be slightly bent. Lower the bar to the floor, using your legs, keeping your shoulders over the bar and your back flat. Keep the bar close to your body and your butt down until the bar reaches the floor.

Figure 4.37 Power Clean finish

High Pull Finish

6. As the bar reaches your upper chest (figure 4.37d), slightly bend your knees to prevent back strain.

7. Slowly lower the bar, keeping it close to your body. To prevent lower back strain, as the bar descends it should brush your thighs and your knees should be slightly bent. Lower the bar to the floor, using your legs, keeping your shoulders over the bar and your back flat. Keep the bar close to your body and your butt down until the bar reaches the floor.

Figure 4.37 High Pull finish

Combo Lift

Hang Clean

1. Stand with your feet hip-width apart, bar near your shins.
2. Grip the bar in a closed pronated shoulder-width grip, palms turned toward your body.
3. Slowly stand up with the bar, keeping it close to your body. Keep your head and shoulders up. Use your legs to lift the weight. Maintain a tight, flat back and straight arms.
4. Cock the bar and slide it down your thighs to the power pulling position, just above your knees.
5. Initiate the pull by explosively extending your legs, hips, and back, keeping your arms straight. Thrust your shoulders back and up. Thrust your hips forward and up.
6. Straighten your legs and extend up onto your toes before your arms begin pulling. Keep the bar close to your body.
7. As the bar reaches your upper chest, lower your body to a one-eighth to one-quarter squat position before the bar starts to descend in preparation for the catching or racking of the bar on your shoulders. Rotate your wrists back around and under the bar, lifting your elbows high out in front of the bar. Carry the bar on your shoulders, knees slightly bent to cushion the impact.
8. Stand with the bar racked on your shoulders. After completing the Hang Clean, begin the Front Squat.

Note:

The Hang Clean can be viewed on the DVD. See figure 4.36 for the starting position.

Front Squat

9. Keep your eyes, head, shoulders, and chest up and maintain a tight back throughout the lift (figure 4.38*a*).

Figure 4.38   Combo Lift: Front Squat

10. Squat down under control, leading with your hips, until your thighs are parallel to the ground (figure 4.38*b*). Do not bounce at the bottom of the movement. Keep your knees in line with your toes; don't allow your knees to move inside or outside the normal tracking of the knee joint or move out in front of your toes. Keep your weight evenly distributed over your feet; do not shift your weight forward to your toes.

11. Raise the bar by straightening your hips and knees while maintaining correct body position. Keep your hips underneath you; do not round your back or lean forward on your feet. After completing the Front Squat, begin the Push Press.

Figure 4.38   Combo Lift: Front Squat

Push Press

12. Perform a one-eighth to one-quarter squat while maintaining a tight, flat back as the bar rests on the front part of your shoulders (figure 4.38*c*).

13. Explosively extend your legs as your hips come forward, up, and through as you push the bar with your arms straight up overhead (figure 4.38*d*). Reach complete lockout in one explosive motion with slightly bent knees as a safety cushion.

14. Return the bar under control to the original starting position on the front of your shoulders, using your legs as a cushion.

15. Slowly lower the bar, keeping it close to your body. To prevent lower back strain, as the bar descends it should brush your thighs and your knees should be slightly bent. Stand straight up with your arms straight and the bar hanging close to your body. After completing the Push Press, begin the Straight-Leg Deadlift.

Figure 4.38   Combo Lift: Push Press

Straight-Leg Deadlift

16. With legs straight or slightly bent (figure 4.38*e*), slowly bend over, keeping your back straight, and lower the bar along your legs to the tops of your feet (figure 4.38*f*). Do not round your back. Do not bang the weight on the floor or bounce at the bottom of the movement.

17. Slowly return to a full standing position, keeping your back straight.

18. Repeat the Hang Clean, Front Squat, Push Press, Straight-Leg Deadlift sequence for the desired number of repetitions; 1 full sequence is 1 repetition.

Figure 4.38   Combo Lift: Straight-Leg Deadlift

19. On the last repetition, lower the bar, keeping it close to your body. Keep your head and shoulders up, arms straight, and back flat and tight. Use your legs to lower the bar under control to the ground.

Leg Press

1. Lie in the leg press or hip sled machine with your back flat and your butt touching the pad.

2. Use the handles to pull your butt up against the pad and hold this position, especially when your legs are at the bottom of the lift.

3. Release the safety catches and turn them out while raising the weight until your legs are almost locked out but not completely.

4. Lower the weight until your legs and thighs have a 75- to 90-degree angle between them (figure 4.39). At the bottom of the lift, knees should not be in front of the toes; if they are, place your feet higher on the foot platform or pedals. Keep your butt on the pad and your back flat at all times. If your butt leaves the pad at the bottom of the lift, it could cause your spine and back to curl up, leading to potential injury.

5. Slowly push the weight back up almost to full extension but not quite.

6. After the last repetition, turn in the safety catches and slowly lower the weight.

Figure 4.39

Lying Hamstring Curl

1. Lie facedown on the hamstring curl machine with your heels under the pads. Hold on to the handles if available.

2. Curl your legs up (figure 4.40). Stay flat on the bench until the pads touch or almost touch your butt or the backs of your thighs.

3. Slowly return to the starting position.

4. Repeat for the desired number of repetitions.

Variation: You can perform the Lying Hamstring Curl one leg at a time.

Figure 4.40

DVD Step-Up

1. The bench, platform, or step required for this exercise should be high enough so your thigh is parallel to the floor when you step up onto it. This exercise can be done with a barbell, dumbbells, or body weight.

2. Start in a standing position, facing the bench or platform. If using dumbbells, hold the dumbbells at your sides. If using a barbell, begin with the barbell on the back of your shoulders.

3. With your right leg, step up onto the bench or platform (figure 4.41*a*). Then lift your left (trailing) leg up and stand on the bench or platform (figure 4.41*b*).

4. Step down under control, right leg first and left leg following.

5. Repeat this sequence, beginning with your left leg. Alternate right-leg, left-leg step-ups until the set is complete.

Figure 4.41

Lunge

1. This exercise can be done with a barbell, dumbbells, or body weight.
2. Start in a standing position. If using dumbbells, hold the dumbbells at your sides. If using a barbell, begin with the barbell on the back of your shoulders.
3. Step forward with your right leg, keeping your head, shoulders, and torso straight up and vertical to the ground. Keep shoulders and hips square as you maintain your balance.

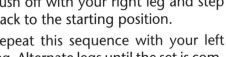

4. Lunge forward until your thigh is parallel to the ground and your shin is straight up and down (figure 4.42). Keep your trailing leg as straight as possible without touching your knee to the floor.
5. Push off with your right leg and step back to the starting position.
6. Repeat this sequence with your left leg. Alternate legs until the set is complete.

Figure 4.42

Side Lunge

1. This exercise can be done with a barbell, dumbbells, or body weight.
2. Start in a standing position. If using dumbbells, hold the dumbbells at your sides or in front of you. If using a barbell, begin with the barbell on the back of your shoulders.
3. Step to the side with your right leg, keeping your head, shoulders, and torso upright until your thigh is almost parallel to the floor (figure 4.43). Your trailing leg should be straight.

4. Push off with your right leg and step back to the starting position.
5. Repeat this sequence with your left leg. Alternate legs until the set is complete.

Figure 4.43

Leg Extension

1. Sit on a leg extension machine with the pads on your shins just above your feet.
2. Your knees should be at the edge of the seat pad with room to move.
3. Legs should be at least vertical to the floor, maybe a little farther back under the seat but not too far. Having your legs too far under the seat will put extra pressure on your knees.
4. Use the handles and belt, if needed.
5. Raise your legs to a fully extended position (figure 4.44) and then lower, maintaining control.

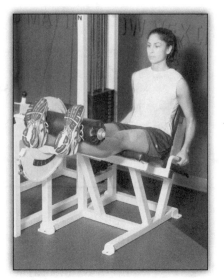

Figure 4.44

Standing Single-Leg Hamstring Curl

1. Stand in front of the standing hamstring curl machine with the lower pad behind and just above your heel and the upper pad against the front of your thigh.
2. Lift your leg toward your butt, keeping your thigh on the upper pad (figure 4.45). If possible, touch the pad to your butt at the top of the movement.
3. Lower the weight under control, keeping your thigh on the upper pad.
4. You can perform all repetitions with 1 leg first and then switch legs or alternate legs with each repetition to complete the set.

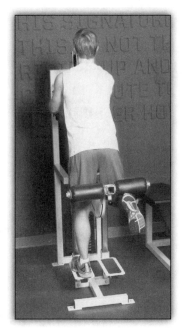

Figure 4.45

Hip Adduction

1. Sit in the adduction machine with your legs apart and the pads resting against your inner thighs or legs. You can adjust how wide your legs are to start with; start as wide as possible. Hold on to the handles.

2. Slowly squeeze your thighs together until the pads touch (figure 4.46).

3. Slowly return to the starting position.

4. If an adduction machine isn't available, you can perform the same exercise using a multihip machine, single-leg low pulley machine, cable machine, or tubing.

Figure 4.46

Hip Abduction

1. Sit on the abduction machine, legs together, pads against your outer thighs or legs. Hold on to the handles.

2. Spread your thighs out as far as possible, pushing against the pads (figure 4.47).

3. Slowly return to the starting position.

4. If an abduction machine is not available, you can perform the exercise using a multihip machine, single-leg low pulley machine, cable machine, or tubing.

Figure 4.47

Straight-Leg Deadlift

1. Stand with feet hip-width apart, holding the bar at thigh level in front of you with arms straight.
2. Grip the bar in a closed pronated shoulder-width grip, palms turned toward your body.
3. With legs straight or slightly bent, slowly bend over, keeping your back straight, and lower the bar along your legs to the tops of your feet. Do not round your back. Do not bang the weight on the floor or bounce at the bottom of the movement.
4. Slowly return to the starting position, keeping your back straight.

Note: For photos of the Straight-Leg Deadlift, please refer to the Combo Lift, page 98.

 ## Back Extension

1. On a back extension bench, place your heels under the heel pads or strap and your thighs on the thigh pad or strap with enough room to bend over.
2. Start at the bottom position with your torso vertical to the ground and your hands behind your head.
3. Raise your torso up with a straight back until it is parallel to the ground or slightly above the thigh pad or strap (figure 4.48).
4. Slowly return to the starting position, keeping your back straight.
5. Control both the raising and lowering phases. Don't hyperextend your lower back too much at the top.

Figure 4.48

Standing Calf Raise

1. Stand with your feet on the standing calf machine platform, heels down, calves stretched, and body straight. The pads are on your shoulders (figure 4.49a).

2. Raise on your toes as high as possible and hold for a count (figure 4.49b).

3. Return to the starting position for a count. The only joint movement is from the ankles.

4. You can work both calves together or 1 calf at a time. When working 1 calf at a time, be sure to switch legs to complete the set.

Figure 4.49

Barbell Bench Press

1. Lie flat on the bench press bench with your head, shoulders, and butt touching the bench. Feet are flat and planted firmly on the floor. Maintain this position throughout the lift.

2. Your head should be not quite underneath the bar; this will prevent the bar from hitting the rack during the exercise. You may need help in getting the bar out of and back into the rack.

3. Your grip on the barbell can vary; in general, it should be slightly wider than shoulder width.

4. The spotter holds the bar in an alternating grip. On the count of 3, the spotter helps you lift the barbell from the rack as you begin the exercise. After helping you get the bar to the starting position, the spotter releases the bar.

5. Slowly lower the bar to your nipple area (4 to 6 in., or 10 to 15 cm, range on your chest). Although grooves vary, the 4- to 6-inch range should fit everyone. Gently touch the bar to your chest without bouncing it, and push it back up to full extension.

6. During the exercise, the spotter will shadow the bar with his hands while not touching the bar unless needed. When you are finished with your repetitions, the spotter will help you rerack the bar.

Note: Refer to Test 5: Bench Press (Maximum Repetitions) on page 8 in chapter 1 for photos showing how to perform the Bench Press.

Dumbbell Bench Press

1. After removing the dumbbells from the rack, sit on the weight bench, placing the dumbbells on your thighs. Use your thighs to help lift the dumbbells to the starting position.

2. Lie flat on the bench with your head, shoulders, and butt touching the bench. Feet are flat and planted firmly on the floor. Maintain this position throughout the lift.

3. Arms and elbows are down with the dumbbells touching your anterior deltoids, similar to a barbell position.

4. Press both dumbbells to a fully extended position over your chest and gently touch them together (figure 4.50). Try to press each arm at the same speed and exercise groove. Slowly lower the dumbbells in the same exercise groove back to the starting position. Controlling the dumbbells is very important.

Figure 4.50

5. After the last repetition, finish with the dumbbells over your chest. Lower them to your thighs as you rock up off the bench. Don't drop the dumbbells; this could cause injury or damage the equipment.

6. Dumbbells may float inside, outside, below, or above the correct exercise groove. The spotter should spot the dumbbells from behind by grabbing the wrists and guiding, if necessary.

Barbell Incline Bench Press

1. Lie on the incline bench press bench with your head, shoulders, and butt touching the bench. Feet are flat and planted firmly on the floor. Maintain this position throughout the lift.

2. Use a medium to wide grip because the exercise grooves on the incline bench are different from those on the bench press.

3. With the help of a spotter, unrack the bar and move it into an overhead starting position, using the same spotting technique as on the bench press.

4. Slowly lower the bar to your upper chest, just below your clavicles (collarbones), and gently touch the bar to your upper chest without bouncing. Push the bar up to full extension (figure 4.51). The incline exercise groove is higher on the chest than the exercise groove on the Bench Press.

Figure 4.51

5. During the exercise, the spotter will shadow the bar with his hands while not touching the bar unless needed. When you are finished with your repetitions, the spotter will help you rerack the bar.

Dumbbell Incline Bench Press

1. Adjust the weight bench so that it has an incline of about 45 degrees.

2. After removing the dumbbells from the rack, sit on the incline weight bench, placing the dumbbells on your thighs. Lift one knee and dumbbell at a time up to your chest to the starting position. Dumbbells should be touching your anterior deltoids, and arms and elbows are down.

3. Lie on the bench with your head, shoulders, and butt in contact with the bench, feet firmly planted on the floor. Maintain this position throughout the lift.

4. Press both dumbbells to the fully extended position over your chest and gently touch them together. Try to press each arm at the same speed and exercise groove. Slowly lower the dumbbells in the same exercise groove back to the starting position (figure 4.52). Controlling the dumbbells is very important.

5. After the last repetition, finish with the dumbbells over your chest. Lower them to your thighs then get up off the bench. Don't drop the dumbbells; this could cause injury or damage the equipment.

6. Dumbbells may float inside, outside, below, or above the correct exercise groove. The spotter should spot the dumbbells from behind by grabbing the wrists and guiding, if necessary.

Figure 4.52

Push Press

1. Place the bar on the rack just under the height of your shoulders so that you have to squat slightly to place the bar on the front part of your shoulders.

2. Approach the rack and grab the bar with a closed pronated shoulder-width grip.

3. Squat under the bar, positioning it on the front part of your shoulders with your elbows up high and out in front of the bar. Straighten your legs and remove the bar from the rack.

4. Step back, allowing yourself enough room away from the rack to perform the exercise safely.

5. Your feet should be shoulder-width apart or slightly wider with your toes pointed straight ahead or slightly out. Look straight ahead.

6. Perform a one-eighth to one-quarter squat while maintaining a tight, flat back as the bar rests on the front part of your shoulders (figure 4.53a).

7. Explosively extend your legs as your hips come forward, up, and through as you push the bar with your arms straight up overhead (figure 4.53b). Reach complete lockout in one explosive motion with slightly bent knees as a safety cushion.

8. Return the bar under control to the original starting position on the front of your shoulders, using your legs as a cushion. Repeat this technique for additional repetitions.

9. When the set is finished, walk all the way into the rack until the bar touches the rack and then squat down until the bar rests on the rack.

Figure 4.53

Standing Military Press

1. Place the bar on the rack just under the height of your shoulders so that you have to squat slightly to place the bar on the front part of your shoulders.

2. Approach the rack and grab the bar with a closed pronated shoulder-width grip.

3. Squat under the bar, positioning it on the front part of your shoulders with your elbows up high and out in front of the bar. Straighten your legs and remove the bar from the rack.

Figure 4.54

4. Step back, allowing yourself enough room away from the rack to perform the exercise safely.

5. Your feet should be shoulder-width apart or slightly wider with your toes pointed straight ahead or slightly out. Look straight ahead (figure 4.54a).

6. Press the bar to full extension over your head without arching your back (figure 4.54b).

7. Lower the bar under control to your shoulders.

8. When you finish the set, walk all the way into the rack until the bar touches the rack and then squat down until the bar rests on the rack.

Seated Dumbbell Shoulder Press

1. Sit on the end of a weight bench or an adjustable weight bench set at a 90-degree angle with your back straight and your feet firmly planted on the floor.

2. Either curl up or lift the dumbbells with one thigh at a time, raising them to the starting position. Dumbbells should be just over your outside shoulders.

3. Press both dumbbells overhead and gently touch them together without arching your back (figure 4.55).

4. Lower the dumbbells under control to the starting position.

5. Dumbbells may float inside, outside, below, or above the correct exercise groove. The spotter should spot the dumbbells from behind by grabbing the wrists and guiding, if necessary.

Figure 4.55

Triceps Press-Down

1. Grip the bar of a high-pulley cable machine, palms down, hands 6 to 10 inches (15 to 25 cm) apart.

2. Keep your arms and elbows fixed and in at your sides.

3. Begin with the bar at about armpit level.

4. Smoothly press the bar down to full extension, moving only your forearms (figure 4.56).

5. Return under control to the starting position.

Figure 4.56

Lying Triceps Extension

1. Lie flat on the bench with your head, shoulders, and butt touching the bench. Feet are flat and planted firmly on the floor. Maintain this position throughout the lift.

2. Hold a cambered curl bar with a closed pronated narrow grip.

3. Begin with the bar extended overhead.

4. Slowly lower the bar toward your forehead, keeping your elbows in (figure 4.57).

5. Extend the bar to a full lockout position over your shoulders. Only your forearms should move. Your arms should be fixed in a vertical, straight, up-and-down position.

6. You can immediately follow this exercise with 10 quick Bench Presses (page 105) using a close grip.

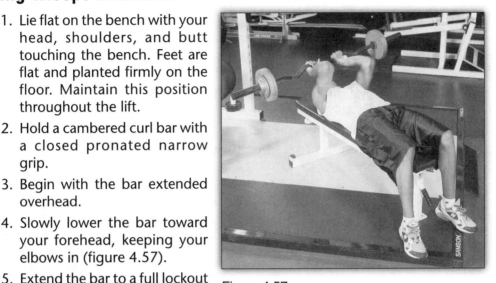

Figure 4.57

Bar Dip

1. Begin on bar dip bars in a straight-arm, locked-out position, supporting your body weight with your body erect.

2. Lower your body under control with elbows in and behind you until your shoulders drop below your elbows (figure 4.58). A 90-degree angle between the arm and forearm is the minimum depth.

3. Press back up to a fully extended position with straight arms.

Figure 4.58

Pull-Up, Wide Grip Behind the Head

1. Hang from a pull-up bar, hands wider than shoulders; hold on to the bar with a pronated grip, palms facing away. Body and arms are straight.
2. Pull up until the back of your neck touches the bar (figure 4.59). Keep your legs fairly straight and don't jerk your body.
3. Slowly return to the starting hanging position with straight arms.

Figure 4.59

Pull-Up, Medium Grip in Front

1. Hang from a pull-up bar with hands slightly wider than shoulder width; hold on to the bar with a pronated grip, palms facing away. Body and arms are straight.
2. Pull up until your chin clears the bar (figure 4.60). Keep your legs fairly straight and don't jerk your body.
3. Slowly return to the starting hanging position with straight arms.

Figure 4.60

Wide-Grip Lat Pulldown Behind Head

1. Sit on the bench of a lat pulldown machine with your legs underneath the thigh pads, if available. Keep your torso vertical to the floor.
2. Hold the bar in a wide pronated grip, palms facing away with straight arms.
3. Pull the bar straight down, without moving your torso, until the bar touches the back of your neck (figure 4.61).
4. Return the bar under control to the starting position.

Figure 4.61

Narrow-Grip Lat Pulldown in Front

1. Sit on the bench of a lat pulldown machine with your legs underneath the thigh pads, if available. Keep your torso vertical to the floor.
2. Hold the bar in a narrow pronated grip, palms facing away, hands shoulder-width apart with straight arms (figure 4.62*a*).
3. Pull the bar straight down, without moving your torso, to just below your chin (figure 4.62*b*).
4. Return the bar under control to the starting position.

Figure 4.62

Low Pulley Seated Lat Row

1. Sit on the pad of a low pulley machine with your legs slightly bent and your feet against the bar or pedals.
2. With your torso in a forward leaning position, grab the handles with straight arms.
3. Pull back on the handles, bringing them to your lower chest or abdomen (figure 4.63). Your torso moves from a forward lean to a slightly backward lean during the pulling phase; keep your knees bent.
4. Slowly return to the starting position.

Figure 4.63

Dumbbell Lat Row

1. Place your right knee and right hand on a flat weight bench with your torso parallel to the floor. Your left leg is out from the bench with a slightly bent knee.
2. Hold a dumbbell in your left hand, arm straight down and hanging at your side (figure 4.64a).
3. Pull the dumbbell up toward the outside of your shoulder with a high elbow at the top of the pull (figure 4.64b).

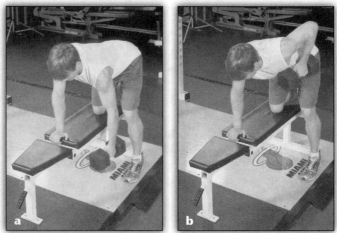

Figure 4.64

Touch the dumbbell to your shoulder. Don't jerk the weight; use a steady pull.

4. Slowly lower the weight to the starting position.

5. After the set is complete with your left arm, repeat the sequence with your right arm.

Lateral Shoulder Fly

1. Sit in a lateral shoulder fly machine with your feet firmly planted on the floor. Position your arms so the pads are against your arms or forearms.

2. Raise your forearms and elbows to above your shoulders (figure 4.65).

3. Slowly return to the starting position.

Figure 4.65

Dumbbell Upright Row

1. Stand with your arms straight, holding the dumbbells against your thighs, thumbs facing each other.

2. Pull the dumbbells straight up your body, without swinging them away from the body, to just below chin level with high elbows at the top of the pull (figure 4.66). Knees are slightly bent.

3. Slowly lower the dumbbells under control to the starting position.

Figure 4.66

Barbell Upright Row

1. Stand with your arms straight, holding the barbell against your thighs, thumbs facing each other. Your hands should be 4 to 8 inches (10 to 20 cm) apart in a closed pronated grip.

2. Pull the barbell straight up the body, without swinging it away from the body, to just below chin level with high elbows at the top of the pull (figure 4.67). Knees are slightly bent.

3. Slowly lower the bar under control to the starting position.

Figure 4.67

Seated Dumbbell Lateral Raise

1. Sit on the end of the weight bench with your back straight and your feet firmly planted on the floor. Hold the dumbbells at your sides with your arms straight and your palms facing in.

2. Raise the dumbbells out to your sides with your knuckles up and elbows slightly bent to just above shoulder height (figure 4.68).

3. Pause at the top of the movement and lower the dumbbells under control to the starting position.

Variation: You can also do this exercise from a standing position with knees slightly bent.

Figure 4.68

Seated Alternating Dumbbell Curl

1. Sit on the end of the weight bench with your back straight and your feet firmly planted on the floor. Hold the dumbbells at your sides with your arms straight and your palms facing in.

2. Curl up one dumbbell until it is past your thigh, then rotate your hand to a supinated (palm-up) position and continue to lift the dumbbell to the front of your shoulder (figure 4.69).

3. Don't swing the dumbbell up. Keep your elbow at your side.

4. Lower the dumbbell under control to the starting position.

5. Repeat with the other arm and continue to alternate arms until the set is complete.

Figure 4.69

Standing Curl Bar Curl

1. Stand with your feet hip-width apart and your knees slightly bent.

2. Hold a cambered curl bar with a supinated grip, palms facing away, with your hands on the angle of the cambered bar. Your arms are straight with the bar resting against your thighs.

3. Curl the bar up, keeping your elbows at your sides until your hands are in front of your shoulders at the top of the lift (figure 4.70). Don't swing the bar or let your elbows move away from your sides.

Figure 4.70

4. Slowly lower the bar to the starting position.

GUIDELINES FOR SETS AND REPETITIONS

There are as many different programs as there are athletes. The age groups we have targeted are high school and older. In general, younger athletes should lift lighter weights with higher repetitions (10 to 20) per set for safety and health reasons.

We have put together a 12-Week Off-Season Strength Training Cycle that provides a logical progression for sets and repetitions for all upper- and lower-body exercises. This progression is based on research that has been done in the strength training field in recent years. Table 4.2 identifies the 6 major phases of progression for strength training, the sets and repetitions for each phase, and the intensity and volume for each phase.

Table 4.2 Six Phases of Strength Training

	Phases					
	Preparation	Hypertrophy	Basic Strength	Strength and Power	In-Season Maintenance	Active Rest
Sets	2-3	3-4	3-4	3-4	3	1-2
Repetitions	15-20	8-12	4-6	2-3	10-8-6	15-20
Intensity	Low	Moderate	High	High	Moderate	Low
Volume	High	High	Moderate	Low	Moderate	High

The following are brief explanations of the 6 major phases of strength training progressions.

The **Preparation Phase** is the beginning phase of a strength training program. The purpose is to help build a muscular endurance conditioning base to prepare the body safely for the higher-intensity strength training phases that will follow. The training intensity is low and the volume is high during this preparation phase.

The **Hypertrophy Phase** is important because it prepares athletes in two major ways for the higher-intensity phases to come later in the cycle:

1. Hypertrophy is the increase in muscle tissue as a result of specific physiological adaptations to training. Increases in muscle tissue improve the chances of developing strength and power.

2. Athletes' anaerobic capacity, or specific endurance related to weight room exercises and workouts, will improve. This improved anaerobic capacity will also help in the later phases of the training cycle, allowing athletes to better handle the higher intensities.

The **Basic Strength Phase** is between the Hypertrophy Phase and the Strength and Power Phase. Increases in strength development in all of the major lifts occur in this phase. The training intensity is high for this phase as increases in both strength and intensity help prepare for the Strength and Power Phase.

The **Strength and Power Phase** has higher intensities and decreases in volume. This aids in the continued strength and power development by lowering the repetitions and focusing on target sets without the fatigue associated with higher-repetition phases. This is also known as the Peaking Phase.

The **In-Season Maintenance Phase** is designed to help athletes maintain as much of the strength and power gained in the off-season as possible throughout the season. There are many in-season programs depending on many variables; listed later in the chapter are the basic adjustments and options for in-season strength training.

The **Active Rest Phase** is also called the postseason. This is the 2- to 8-week time period immediately following the season. The length will vary depending on your situation. During this time the body and mind should recover from the stresses placed on them during the season. Activities should be low in intensity and high in volume to allow the body to recover while still being somewhat active. Two light workouts a week with 1 or 2 sets of 15 to 20 repetitions per exercise is a good parameter. Circuits may also be done at this time. It is a good idea during active rest to do some cross-training in different sports activities as well, but keep the intensity low.

STRENGTH TRAINING PROGRAMS

Each strength training program should be designed with an individual athlete in mind. Each program should address specific strengths, weaknesses, priorities, needs, and target areas. Of course, we cannot prescribe individual programs for you, but we show you 7 programs with options that will fit the needs of almost every athlete, regardless of sex, age, ability, or experience:

Off-Season:

Four-Day Split Program

Three-Day Total-Body Program

In-Season:

Total-Body Program

Lower-Body Program

Upper-Body Program

Total-Body Circuit Program

Combo Program

Each of these programs uses functional exercises for basketball that will also enhance proper muscle balance as it relates to movement efficiency and injury reduction. Each program has 1 to 3 recovery days between workouts. Research shows the best recovery time for muscle repair and replenishment to be 48 to 96 hours, depending on many variables.

Off-Season Strength Training Programs

The two off-season strength training programs are the Four-Day Split Program and the Three-Day Total-Body Program.

Four-Day Split Program

This program may be used by the beginner, intermediate, or advanced athlete. This design allows a 2- to 3-day recovery time between workouts for the same muscle groups and allows you to focus on one body segment per workout, upper body or lower body (table 4.3). The workouts may be shorter depending on whether you superset and how many exercises you perform.

Table 4.3 12-Week Off-Season Strength Training Four-Day Split Program

Lower body: Monday and Thursday	Upper body: Tuesday and Friday
1. Hang Clean or Hang Pull	1. Bench Press 1. Pull-Up or Lat Pulldown
2. Squat or Leg Press 2. Hamstring Curl	2. Incline Bench Press 2. Seated Lat Row or Dumbbell Lat Row
3. Lunge, Step-Up, or Leg Extension 3. Straight-Leg Deadlift or Back Extension	3. Shoulder Press (bar or dumbbell, seated or standing) (first 6 weeks); Push Press (second 6 weeks) 3. Upright Row or Dumbbell Lateral Raise
4. Side Lunge or Abduction, Adduction 4. Standing Calf Raise	4. Bar Dip or Triceps Press-Down 4. Biceps Curl
5. Core—lower back 5. Core—abs	5. Core—abs

The workout days are Monday and Thursday, Tuesday and Friday. You may choose what days (Monday and Thursday or Tuesday and Friday) to work either the upper body or the lower body. This program is also forgiving. If you miss a day, you should still have enough open days to get all your workouts in. It is designed to superset the exercises with the same number on the workout cards in chapter 8. These exercises either work opposing muscle groups or are exercises that will not interfere with each other but actually enhance each other. The following are some advantages of supersetting:

- Faster workouts
- Proper muscle balance
- Increased conditioning levels
- Cleaner neuromuscular signal, recruitment, and function
- Increased blood flow to body segments being exercised

Sets and repetitions are listed on the 12-Week Off-Season Strength Training Cycle for this program (tables 4.5 and 4.6, pages 125 and 126). Workout cards for this program are provided in chapter 8, page 193.

Three-Day Total-Body Program

This program may also be used by the beginner, intermediate, or advanced athlete. It is designed for the player who has only 3 days during the week to strength train. You may do this program Monday, Wednesday, and Friday or Tuesday, Thursday, and Saturday. Allow 1 day in between workouts. The Wednesday workout works the same muscle groups as the Monday and Friday workouts, but it uses different exercises (table 4.4).

The Monday and Friday workouts start with the lower-body exercises first and the Wednesday workout starts with the upper body. This program

Table 4.4 12-Week Off-Season Strength Training Three-Day Total-Body Program

Monday and Friday	Wednesday
1. Hang Clean	1. Dumbbell Bench Press 1. Pull-Up
2. Squat or Leg Press 2. Hamstring Curl	2. Dumbbell Incline Bench Press 2. Dumbbell Lat Row or Seated Lat Row
3. Step-Up or Leg Extension 3. Straight-Leg Deadlift	3. Dumbbell Lateral Raise 3. Bar Dip 3. Bar Biceps Curl
4. Side Lunge or Abduction, Adduction 4. Standing Calf Raise	4. Hang Pull
5. Bench Press 5. Lat Pulldown	5. Lunge 5. Hamstring Curl
6. Push Press	6. Standing Calf Raise 6. Back Extension
7. Triceps Press-Down 7. Dumbbell Biceps Curl	7. Core—abs 7. Core—lower back
8. Core—abs 8. Core—lower back	

may take a little longer because each workout is total body. You may speed up the workouts by supersetting the same numbered exercises on the workout cards in chapter 8.

Sets and repetitions are listed in the 12-Week Off-Season Strength Training Cycle for this program (tables 4.5 and 4.6, pages 125 and 126). Workout cards for this program are provided in chapter 8, page 195.

In-Season Strength Training Programs

The 5 In-Season Strength Training Programs are Total-Body Program, Four-Day Split Lower-Body Program, Four-Day Split Upper-Body Program, Total-Body Circuit Program, and Combo Program.

In-Season Strength Training Program Options

1. In-season programs cut back on the number of exercises per body part, usually only 1 exercise per muscle group is done.

2. Try to do 2 strength training workouts per body part each week during the in-season. If you have 2 days or more before your next game, you may lift heavier, following the suggested 10-8-6 sets and repetitions, or split the lower- and upper-body workouts into 2 days (lower body 2 days before a game and upper body 1 day before a game). If you have only 1 day off in between games, you may lift lighter following

the same 10-8-6, or you may do 3 × 15, 15-12-10, 3 × 10, and so on. You may also lift lighter by doing only 2 sets of each exercise or fewer exercises per workout.

3. On lighter lifting days, you may substitute exercises. For example, Leg Press instead of Squat, Straight-Leg Deadlift instead of Hang Clean, and Machine or Dumbbell Bench Press instead of Bench Press.

4. You may speed up the workouts for in-season (Total Body, Lower Body, Upper Body) by supersetting the same numbered exercises on the workout cards in chapter 8.

5. For a quick Total-Body Workout option, you may do a Total-Body Circuit Program.

6. For a quick power workout, use the Combo Program option.

7. Depending on game, practice, and travel schedules, there may be time for only 1 Lower-Body Workout some weeks.

In general, in-season programs should have fewer exercises and a reduced frequency and level of intensity compared to the off-season program. High-risk lifts or lifts that require certain techniques should be adjusted or eliminated during the in-season as well. These adjustments are made to avoid overtraining between practices, games, and workouts; overtraining may lead to decreased performance or injury.

Following are the brief descriptions of the programs for In-Season Strength Training. Please refer to the section titled In-Season Strength Training Program Options, which explains in greater detail the days, exercises, sets, repetitions, and supersetting.

Total-Body Program

This program includes exercises that work the major muscle groups of your total body in 1 strength training workout. Follow the In-Season Total-Body Program card in chapter 8 (page 197) for 2 days per week.

This program may take a little longer, and you can make it quicker by performing only 1 exercise per body part, supersetting, or doing only 2 sets per exercise instead of 3.

Lower-Body Program

This program focuses on the major muscle groups of the lower body and core only. You may use the Four-Day Split Lower-Body Program card in chapter 8 (page 193) or the In-Season Total-Body Program card (lower-body and core exercises only) in chapter 8 (page 197). You may also quicken the workout by performing only 1 exercise per body part, supersetting, or doing only 2 sets per exercise instead of 3.

Upper-Body Program

This program focuses on the major muscle groups of the upper body and core only. You may use the Four-Day Split Upper-Body Program card in chapter 8 (page 194) or the In-Season Total-Body Program card (upper-body and core exercises only) in chapter 8 (page 197). You may also quicken the workout by performing only 1 exercise per body part, supersetting, or doing only 2 sets per exercise instead of 3.

Total-Body Circuit Program

This program includes 12 exercise stations that work the major muscle groups of the total body in 1 strength training workout. Muscular endurance and conditioning are the focus of this workout. Each exercise station is 30 seconds of work. You should choose a weight with a goal of achieving 15 quality repetitions per set. If your first set was too easy, increase the weight on the second set for that exercise. If it was too hard and you could not get 15 repetitions, reduce the weight for the second set of that exercise. The goal is to increase the weight for each set of the circuit. You will have 30 seconds between exercises to get to the next station and adjust the weights and the machine for your individual needs before the next 30-second exercise time period. Use the In-Season Total-Body Circuit Program card in chapter 8 (page 198) and follow the proper exercise order listed (1 to 12) if you do the circuit by yourself. If more than one athlete is doing the circuit at the same time, follow the exercise order through to your original starting station. Do the entire circuit for 2 or 3 sets depending on your time. Two sets of the circuit will take 24 minutes and 3 sets will take 36 minutes.

Combo Program

This program incorporates many of the major muscle groups in a combination of various explosive-type movements to train your body effectively in a short period of time. The emphasis of the In-Season Combo Program is strength, power, and some anaerobic conditioning. The exercises are the Hang Clean, Front Squat, Push Press, and Straight-Leg Deadlift in succession.

You may use the Four-Day Split Lower-Body program card in chapter 8 (page 193) or the In-Season Total-Body Program card (lower body) in chapter 8 (page 197) to record your Combo workout. Write "Combo" in the top set box and your 3 sets directly below—5 repetitions, 3 repetitions, 3 repetitions. Please refer to the strength training techniques section for explanations of safe and proper technique for the Combo Lift.

1. After warming up 3 to 5 minutes, begin by performing a Hang Clean (page 93).
2. After a Hang Clean, perform a Front Squat (page 96).
3. After performing a Front Squat, slightly bend your knees and explode up into a Push Press (page 108).
4. Lower the bar to the front of your shoulders first and return it to the original hanging position.

5. Slightly bend your knees while keeping your back tight and flat and perform a Straight-Leg Deadlift (page 98).

6. This total sequence is 1 repetition.

Complete the combo sequence for 5 repetitions for the first set and 3 repetitions for the second and third sets. If time permits, you may do more core abdominal and lower-back exercises.

Postseason

The postseason starts with the Active Rest Phase. This phase is 2 to 8 weeks immediately following the season. Following the Active Rest Phase is the Four-Week Off-Season Preparation Phase before the 12-Week Off-Season Program.

4-Week Off-Season Preparation Phase Program

The Preparation Phase is the 4-week period just before the 12-Week Off-Season Program. It is an important time for developing a muscular endurance conditioning base that will give you an advantage and a head start as you begin the 12-Week Off-Season Program. The Preparation Phase Program is 2 or 3 sets of 15 to 20 repetitions.

Note: The quality of work invested in each training phase will allow for greater gains in the following training phases.

12-Week Off-Season Strength Training Program

The 12-Week Off-Season Cycles match the workout cards in chapter 8 (pages 193-197) except the cycles have the numbers of weeks listed at the top of the page of the prescribed sets and repetitions for each exercise (table 4.5 and table 4.6). Certain exercises have repetitions for high school athletes indicated by HS for that exercise. Players who are college age or older should follow the sets and repetitions listed with the letter C. Players who are younger than high school age should lift lighter weights with higher repetitions (10 to 20) per set.

On the major lifts, such as the Squat, Leg Press, Hang Clean, Bench Press, and Incline Bench Press, the sets and repetitions include target sets only. They do not include warm-up sets. In the target sets, use the heaviest weight possible while maintaining proper technique and performing all of the prescribed repetitions in each set.

The 12-Week Off-Season Cycle starts 12 weeks before the first practice; for best results, please follow the complete program the way it was designed.

Table 4.5 12-Week Off-Season Cycle: Lower-Body Program

Exercises	2 Weeks	2 Weeks	4 Weeks	2 Weeks	2 Weeks
1. Hang Clean or Hang Pull	8-6-6-6 quality sets	8-6-6-4 (C) 8-6-6-6 (HS) quality sets	8-5-5-4 (C) 8-5-5-5 (HS) quality sets	6-4-3-2 (C) 8-5-5-5 (HS) quality sets	6-4-3-2 (C) 8-5-5-5 (HS) quality sets
2. Squat or Leg Press	4 × 10 quality sets	4 × 8 quality sets	4 × 6 quality sets	6-4-3-2 (C) 4 × 6 (HS)	5-3-2-2 (C) 4 × 6 (HS)
2. Hamstring Curl (lying, single-leg, seated, or standing)	4 × 10	4 × 10	10-10-8-8	10-8-6-6	10-8-6-6
3. Lunge, Step-Up, or Leg Extension	3 × 10	3 × 10	10-8-8	10-8-6	10-8-6
3. Straight-Leg Deadlift or Back Extension	3 × 15	3 × 15	3 × 12–15	3 × 12–15	3 × 12–15
4. Side Lunge or Abduction, Adduction	2 × 10–15	2 × 10–15	2 × 10–15	2 × 10–15	2 × 10–15
4. Standing Calf Raise	2 × 15–25	2 × 15–25	2 × 15–25	2 × 15–25	2 × 15–25
5. Core—lower back (pick 2: trunk extension, hip extension, total core)	10–25 each	10–25 each	10–25 each	10–25 each	10–25 each
5. Core—abs (pick 3: trunk flexion, hip flexion, rotary)	10–50 each	10–50 each	10–50 each	10–50 each	10–50 each

C = college level and above; HS = high school level.

Table 4.6 12-Week Off-Season Cycle: Upper-Body Program

Exercises	3 Weeks	2 Weeks	4 Weeks	1 Week	2 Weeks
1. Bench Press (bar, dumbbell or machine)	4 × 10 quality sets	4 × 8 quality sets	4 × 6 quality sets	6-4-3-2 (C) 4 × 6 (HS) quality sets	5-3-2-2 (C) 4 × 6 (HS) quality sets
1. Pull-Up or Lat Pulldown (front or behind)	4 × max. or 4 × 10	4 × max. or 4 × 8 weighted	4 × max. or 10-8-6-10 weighted	4 × max. or 10-8-6-10 weighted	4 × max. or 10-8-6-10 weighted
2. Incline Bench Press (bar, dumbbell, or machine)	3 × 10 quality sets	3 × 8 quality sets	3 × 6 quality sets	6-4-3 (C) 3 × 6 (HS) quality sets	5-3-2 (C) 3 × 6 (HS) quality sets
2. Seated Lat Row or Dumbbell Lat Row	3 × 10	3 × 8	10-8-6	10-8-6	10-8-6
3. Shoulder Press (bar or dumbbell, seated or standing) (first 6 weeks); Push Press (second 6 weeks)	3 × 10	3 × 8	3 × 6	3 × 5	3 × 5
3. Upright Row or Dumbbell Lateral Raise	3 × 10	3 × 10	10-8-8	10-8-10	10-8-10
4. Bar Dip or Triceps Press-Down	3 × max. or 3 × 10 weighted (Bar Dip only); 3 × 10 (Triceps Press-Down only)	3 × max. or 3 × 8 weighted (Bar Dip only); 3 × 10 (Triceps Press-Down only)	3 × max. or 10-8-6 weighted (Bar Dip only); 3 × 10 (Triceps Press-Down only)	3 × max. or 10-8-6 weighted (Bar Dip only); 3 × 10 (Triceps Press-Down only)	3 × max. or 10-8-6 weighted (Bar Dip only); 3 × 10 (Triceps Press-Down only)
4. Biceps Curl (bar or dumbbell)	3 × 10	10-8-8	10-8-8	10-8-6	10-8-6
5. Core—abs (pick 4: trunk flexion, hip flexion, rotary)	10–50 each	10–50 each	10–50 each	10–50 each	10–50 each

C = college level and above; HS = high school level.

* With Pull-Ups and Bar Dips, 3 × max. means body weight repetitions ranging from 2–30+. Weighted Pull-Ups and Bar Dips follow the sets and repetitions listed.

Chapter 5

Power

The ultimate result of plyometric training is to increase an athlete's power. Power is the relationship between strength and speed. The goal of power training is to stimulate the neuromuscular system to alternate quickly from lengthening the muscle (eccentric contraction) to shortening the muscle (concentric contraction) in the shortest amount of time. The term used for this phenomenon is *myotatic stretch reflex*. The myotatic stretch reflex results in the reflex contraction of a muscle after that muscle has been stretched rapidly (as during the eccentric, or loading, phase of a plyometric exercise), leading to powerful and explosive movements.

Powerful basketball players are able to generate maximum force in a short time. Powerful, quick, and explosive movements—such as jump shots, rebounds, passes, and defensive reactions—are key to basketball players' success. Basketball utilizes many different plyometric movements. These powerful movements include forward, backward, lateral, rotational, and vertical movements involving sprints, shuffles, skips, hops, jumps, and passes. Basketball skills are enhanced by participation in a carefully planned, systematic plyometric program.

In the 1960s, Dr. Yuri Verkhoshansky developed a regimen of exercises that introduced explosive training to athletics. The coach of the Soviet track and field jump events organized various hops and jumps into a systematic program he called *shock training*. During that time the Soviet Union and other Eastern bloc countries that dominated the sports world used shock training as an integral part of their preparation for competition. Valery Borzov won the 100-meter dash in the 1972 Olympics and credited his win and drop in time to shock training. Only then were articles discussing this type of jump training published.

In 1975 the great U.S. track and field coach Fred Wilt, who was known for his progressive attitude toward training, referred to this type of shock training as *plyometrics*. The word *plyometrics* is a combination of the Latin roots *plyo* (increase) and *metrics* (measures), reflecting the measurable increase that results from shock training.

In the late 1970s and early 1980s, Dr. Donald Chu became one of the leading authorities and authors on plyometric exercises and their benefits. Some of the information in this chapter is from Chu's book *Jumping Into Plyometrics*.

PLYOMETRIC PREPARATION AND PROGRESSIONS

Athletes' upper- and lower-body strength must be sufficient to safely handle the intensity of plyometric exercises without a breakdown in proper technique. Plyometric exercises are divided into three levels: beginning, intermediate, and advanced. All athletes, male and female, must start at the beginning level. Athletes must be able to perform all beginning drills and exercises with proper technique before progressing to the intermediate exercises. To progress to the advanced exercises, athletes must be able to perform all intermediate exercises with proper technique.

In some situations, athletes have been tested for adequate conditioning before beginning an advanced plyometric exercise program. The following tests have been used to determine an athlete's readiness for highly advanced plyometric exercises. One lower-body test required athletes to perform 5 squats with a load of 60 percent of their body weight before starting a highly advanced program. Another test required that athletes be able to single-leg press their body weight at least 10 times. Eastern bloc countries had athletes perform one squat at 1.5 to 2.0 times their body weight. Upper-body tests for highly advanced plyometrics included a bench press of 1.5 times body weight for males and a bench press of body weight for females.

Note: As you begin a plyometric program, the emphasis on strength training should not be decreased.

PLYOMETRIC TECHNIQUE

Proper technique is crucial to performing plyometric exercises safely and effectively. Understanding how to move the body in the most efficient manner will maximize results and reduce the risk of injury.

Being able to visualize how to start and land is very important. Begin with a mental image of your legs as the shock absorbers in a car. First stand in a quarter-squat position (riding down the road). Then straighten your legs (going over a bump) and return to the quarter-squat position (riding down the road again).

Next, synchronize your arm and leg actions. Stand with your feet hip-width apart and your knees bent in a quarter-squat position. Your arms are back, elbows are bent, and hands are by your hips. During the extension, or jump, phase, drive your hands forward and up to at least shoulder height as your feet leave the ground. Return to the starting position and repeat the cycle. Focus on landing softly.

To work on synchronizing your arm and leg actions, practice multiple repetitions of this plyometric movement without leaving the ground. When you feel ready, go up onto your toes during the extension phase before returning to the starting position. Then perform small jumps while landing softly.

Emphasize proper foot landing in plyometric training. Land on the balls of your feet first and then flatten to your heels with your knees bent. The box circuit is an exception. During the box circuit, land on your heels first and then roll forward to your toes. In the box circuit, the landing pattern should be heels to toes on the boxes, toes to heels on the ground.

As with any type of jumping, proper technique and landing are essential for reducing the risk of injury. Always bend your knees when landing. Your knees should be aligned directly over your toes. Absorb the impact and disperse it throughout the body. Avoid landing straight-legged; this will jar the knees, hips, and back, raising the risk of injury. Because core strength is crucial in protecting the spine from injury, develop and maintain a strong core (back and abdominal muscles). See chapter 4, Strength, for more on training the core.

GUIDELINES FOR PLYOMETRIC DRILLS AND EXERCISES

Plyometric training can be hard on the body. You need to observe several precautions and make sure your participation is properly supervised. Consider the following factors:

1. **Medical history:** Consider any previous injuries. Some circumstances may require a medical release.

2. **Age:** Prepubescent athletes should be strictly supervised. Focus on proper technique and low impact to protect joints and growth plates on bones. Young athletes should perform only low-intensity versions of plyometric drills.

3. **Adequate strength base:** Strength, both upper and lower body, must be sufficient to safely handle the intensity of plyometric exercises.

4. **Footwear:** Select shoes that provide a high degree of lateral stability, arch support, heel cushion, and a nonslip sole, preferably a good basketball shoe.

5. **Surface:** The surface should be solid for maximum response on contact, yet it should have enough give to lessen impact. Quality surfaces include wood basketball courts, rubberized flooring, and tracks.

6. **Equipment:** Equipment must be safe, in good condition, and properly maintained. Boxes should be sturdy and have slightly padded matting

or carpet on top. Be sure the surface of the box is free of any protrusions or seams that may cause injury. Barriers should be soft or break away.

7. **Warm-up and cool-down:** Perform a quality warm-up and cool-down before and after every workout.

8. **Intensity:** Drills should progress in intensity—from beginning to intermediate to advanced—and from two-foot drills to one-foot drills.

9. **Training sequence:** You may perform plyometrics first while fresh or at the end of a workout when fatigued. Some research shows highly advanced athletes and coaches using plyometrics in a fatigued state. Only highly trained athletes should perform plyometrics while fatigued. That is why we recommend doing plyometrics first.

10. **Proper technique:** Follow proper technique when performing any exercise. Careful supervision by trained professionals is strongly recommended. If a breakdown in technique occurs, stop the drill.

PROGRAM DEVELOPMENT

Consider these 5 variables when preparing a quality plyometric program: warm-up and cool-down, intensity, volume, recovery, and frequency.

1. **Warm-up and cool-down:** You should be thoroughly warmed up before beginning plyometric drills and exercises. See chapter 2, Warm-Up and Flexibility, for a quality warm-up and stretching routine. After finishing plyometric training, you need to cool down. The cool-down should include light physical activity and stretching of the lower back, hamstrings, quadriceps, and groin.

2. **Intensity:** The amount of effort required to perform the prescribed exercises should systematically increase. All athletes should move from beginning exercises to intermediate exercises to advanced exercises throughout the 12-Week Off-Season Training Program. Adding exercises, sets, and repetitions; changing the heights of boxes and barriers; and controlling exercise and rest times are all variables of intensity.

3. **Volume:** Consider the total number of foot contacts or jumps performed during a particular session (table 5.1). In general, a beginning athlete will perform fewer foot contacts than an advanced athlete in each category—beginning, intermediate, and advanced exercises. As you progress from beginning to intermediate exercises, you will still perform some of the beginning exercises in each plyometric workout. As you progress from intermediate to advanced exercises, you will still perform some beginning and intermediate exercises as a progression before the advanced exercises. Advanced exercises are more stressful on the body, so we suggest fewer foot contacts in this category. Count the total number of foot contacts in each workout and stay within your designated category (beginning, intermediate, or advanced).

Table 5.1 Suggested Volume for Plyometric Training

Level	Training weeks	Foot contacts (lower body)	Repetitions (upper body)	Sample exercises
Beginning exercises	1-4	100-300	20-30	Quick-feet line drills, Single-Leg Running Hook, Medicine Ball Chest Pass
Intermediate exercises	5-8	100-200	40-50	Box Jump, Power Skip, Medicine Ball Side Pass
Advanced exercises	9-12	50-150	60-70	Depth Jump, Box Circuit, Bounds, Platform Push-Up

In-season plyometric training should be closely monitored and individualized. Since basketball practices and games use many plyometric movements, we recommend limiting in-season plyometrics. A player's practice and game minutes should dictate the type and amount of in-season plyometrics.

4. **Recovery:** Plyometrics is an anaerobic activity. Therefore, the work-to-rest ratio should range from 1:5 to 1:10, depending on the intensity of the exercise. For example, a beginning exercise that takes 10 seconds would need a 50-second recovery. An advanced exercise that takes 10 seconds may need up to 100 seconds of recovery.

5. **Frequency:** A minimum of 72 hours is recommended between training sessions. During the off-season, plyometric training can be done 2 times per week.

PLYOMETRIC EXERCISES

The plyometric exercises that follow are separated into 5 major categories: double leg, single leg, quick feet, upper body, and with a basketball.

A special category of plyometrics, frequently called non-weight bearing, involves unloading a predetermined percentage of a person's body weight. Non-weight-bearing plyometrics benefit prepubescent athletes, injured athletes, and those with weight limit concerns. Non-weight-bearing plyometrics include movements performed in a pool and on a plyometric shuttle. The pool exercises include multidirectional skips, hops, bounds, and jumps with two feet, one foot, and alternating feet. The plyometric shuttle exercises include double-leg, single-leg, and alternating footwork.

Double-Leg Plyometrics

The double-leg plyometric exercises are separated into three major categories: barrier jumps, maximum jumps, and box jumps. Basketball movements that are improved by double-leg plyometric exercises are jump shots, rebounds, and blocking shots.

BARRIER JUMPS

Use small hurdles, foam, or tubing as barriers. Heights and distances of the barriers should be constant to start. Remember to bend your knees on each jump and landing.

Advanced variations of barrier jumps include progressively increasing the height and distance of the barriers with each consecutive jump.

Double-Leg Forward Barrier Jump

Height of barriers: 6 to 24 inches (15 to 60 cm)

Distance between barriers: 2 to 4 feet (60 to 120 cm)

Number of barriers: 6 to 10

1. Stand facing the first barrier with your feet hip-width apart, knees slightly bent, arms back, elbows bent, and hands by your hips.

2. Drive your arms forward and up as you jump forward over each barrier as quickly as possible (figure 5.1).

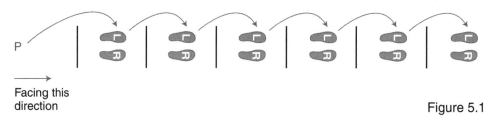

Facing this
direction

Figure 5.1

Double-Leg Lateral Barrier Jump

Height of barriers: 6 to 24 inches (15 to 60 cm)

Distance between barriers: 2 to 4 feet (60 to 120 cm)

Number of barriers: 6 to 10

1. Stand sideways with your right shoulder facing the first barrier and your feet hip-width apart, knees slightly bent, arms back, elbows bent, and hands by your hips.

2. Drive your arms forward and up as you jump laterally to your right over each barrier as quickly as possible (figure 5.2).

3. Repeat, leading with your left shoulder.

Facing this
direction

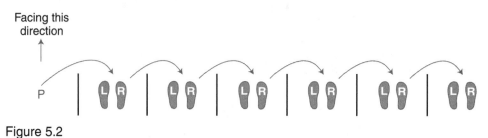

Figure 5.2

Double-Leg Diagonal Barrier Jump

Height of barriers: 6 to 24 inches (15 to 60 cm)

Angles of barrier placement: 30 to 60 degrees (45 degrees is standard)

Number of barriers: 6 to 10

1. Stand on the right side and middle of the first barrier, facing forward with your feet hip-width apart, knees slightly bent, arms back, elbows bent, and hands by your hips.

2. Drive your arms forward and up as you jump to the left and right diagonally over each barrier in a zigzag pattern as quickly as possible (figure 5.3).

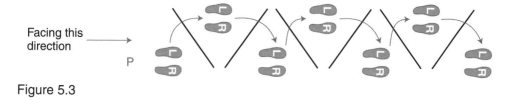

Figure 5.3

MAXIMUM JUMPS

Perform each of these drills with a controlled landing first before advancing to quick consecutive jumps. Remember to bend your knees on each jump and landing.

Double-Leg Hop

1. Stand with your feet shoulder-width apart, knees slightly bent, arms back, elbows bent, and hands by your hips (figure 5.4a).

2. Drive your arms forward and up as you jump forward for maximum height and distance straight ahead for 3 or 4 jumps (figure 5.4b).

Figure 5.4

Knees-to-Chest Jump

1. Stand with your feet shoulder-width apart, knees slightly bent, arms back, elbows bent, and hands by your hips.

2. Drive your arms and knees up, bringing your knees to your chest (figure 5.5) for 10 maximum-height jumps in place.

Figure 5.5

Vertical Jump

1. Stand with your feet shoulder-width apart, knees slightly bent, arms back, elbows bent, and hands by your hips.

2. Drive your arms forward and up as you jump straight up (figure 5.6) for 10 maximum-height jumps in place.

Figure 5.6

BOX JUMPS

For safety, establish proper technique on lower boxes before progressing to higher boxes. Knee angles upon landing on the box must be a minimum of 90 degrees, preferably greater, or the box is too high for you.

Box Jump

Height of box: 18 to 48 inches (45 to 120 cm)

Number of boxes: 1

1. Stand facing the box with your feet hip-width apart, knees slightly bent, arms back, elbows bent, and hands by your hips (figure 5.7a).
2. Drive your arms forward and up as you jump up onto the box (figure 5.7b). Land softly with your feet hip- to shoulder-width apart and your knees bent (figure 5.7c).
3. Step (do not jump) off the back of the box, landing with your feet shoulder-width apart and knees bent.
4. Return to the front of the box and repeat for 8 to 10 jumps.

Figure 5.7

DVD Side-to-Side Box Jump

Height of box: 6 to 18 inches (15 to 45 cm)

Number of boxes: 1

1. Stand sideways to the box with your right shoulder facing the box and your feet hip-width apart, knees slightly bent, arms back, elbows bent, and hands by your hips (figure 5.8*a*).
2. Drive your arms forward and up as you jump up to your right onto the box. Land softly with your feet hip-width apart and knees slightly bent (figure 5.8*b*).
3. Immediately jump off the box to the opposite side in the same landing position (figure 5.8*c*).
4. Quickly jump back to your left onto the box and immediately return to the starting position.
5. Continue this quick touch-and-go pattern for 8 to 10 jumps.

Figure 5.8

Depth Jump

Height of box: 18 to 48 inches (45 to 120 cm)

Number of boxes: 1

A depth jump involves stepping off a predetermined height and, upon landing, immediately jumping. For the purpose of this book, we have included a Box Jump first as a progression to the Depth Jump.

1. Stand facing the box with your feet hip-width apart, knees slightly bent, arms back, elbows bent, and hands by your hips.
2. Drive your arms forward and up as you jump up onto the box. Land softly with your feet hip- to shoulder-width apart and knees bent.
3. Step (do not jump) off the back of the box (figure 5.9a), landing with your feet shoulder-width apart and knees bent (figure 5.9b).
4. Immediately perform a maximum vertical jump straight up (figure 5.9c).
5. Return to the front of the box and repeat for 4 to 6 jumps.

Figure 5.9

Advanced versions: Immediately after stepping off the box and landing,

- perform a Double-Leg Hop for maximum height and distance;
- jump up and over a barrier (tubing, rope, or hurdle); or,
- jump up onto another box.

DVD **Box Circuit**

Height of boxes: 12 to 48 inches (30 to 120 cm)

Distance between boxes: 2 to 4 feet (60 to 120 cm)

Number of boxes: 4 to 6

The heights and distances of the boxes should progressively increase. For example, 12-inch box, 18-inch box, 24-inch box, and 30-inch box (30, 45, 60, and 75 cm). Remember to bend your knees on each jump and landing.

1. Stand facing the first box with your feet hip-width apart, knees slightly bent, arms back, elbows bent, and hands by your hips.
2. Drive your arms forward and up as you jump up onto the box. Land softly with your feet hip- to shoulder-width apart and your knees bent.
3. Step (do not jump) off the back of the box, landing with your feet shoulder-width apart and your knees bent.
4. Immediately jump up onto the next box, landing softly with your feet hip- to shoulder-width apart and your knees bent.
5. Repeat this sequence for the remaining boxes. Do 1 or 2 circuits.

Advanced version: Jump up on and off the boxes quickly in a touch-and-go sequence.

Single-Leg Plyometrics

The single-leg plyometric exercises that follow are separated into three major categories: barrier jumps, maximum jumps, and box jumps. Basketball movements that are improved by single-leg plyometric exercises are layups, dunks, rebounds, and blocking shots. Single-leg plyometric exercises are generally more advanced than double-leg exercises; therefore more caution is advised with proper technique and progressions.

BARRIER JUMPS

Use small hurdles, foam, or tubing as barriers. Heights and distances of the barriers should be constant to start. Remember to bend your knees on each jump and landing.

Advanced variations of barrier jumps include progressively increasing the height and distance of the barriers with each consecutive jump.

Single-Leg Forward Barrier Jump

Height of barriers: 1 to 12 inches (2.5 to 30 cm)

Distance between barriers: 2 to 4 feet (60 to 120 cm)

Number of barriers: 4 to 8

1. Stand facing the first barrier with your feet slightly less than hip-width apart. Stand on your right foot with your right knee slightly bent. Lift your left foot 2 to 6 inches (5 to 15 cm) off the ground and next to your right ankle (with your knee bent). Arms are back, elbows are bent, and hands are by your hips.

2. Drive your arms forward and up as you jump forward over each barrier as quickly as possible on your right foot.

3. Repeat the drill with your left foot.

Single-Leg Lateral Barrier Jump

Height of barriers: 1 to 12 inches (2.5 to 30 cm)

Distance between barriers: 2 to 4 feet (60 to 120 cm)

Number of barriers: 4 to 8

1. Stand sideways to the first barrier with your right shoulder facing the first barrier and your feet slightly less than hip-width apart. Stand on your right foot with your right knee slightly bent. Lift your left foot 2 to 6 inches (5 to 15 cm) off the ground and next to your right ankle (with your knee bent). Your arms are back, elbows are bent, and hands are by your hips.

2. Drive your arms forward and up as you jump laterally over each barrier as quickly as possible on your right foot.

3. Repeat the drill with your left foot.

Single-Leg Diagonal Barrier Jump

Height of barriers: 1 to 12 inches (5 to 30 cm)

Angles of barrier placement: 30 to 60 degrees (45 degrees is standard)

Number of barriers: 6 to 10

1. Stand on the left side and middle of the first barrier with your feet slightly less than hip-width apart. Stand on your right foot with your right knee slightly bent, facing forward. Lift your left foot 2 to 6 inches (5 to 15 cm) off the ground and next to your right ankle (with your knee bent). Your arms are back, elbows are bent, and hands are by your hips.

2. Drive your arms forward and up as you jump to the right and left diagonally over the barriers in a zigzag pattern as quickly as possible on your right foot.

3. Repeat the drill with your left foot.

MAXIMUM JUMPS

Start with smaller hops, skips, and bounds first. Build toward maximum height and distance with each repetition.

Alternating Hop

1. Stand facing forward with your feet slightly less than hip-width apart. Stand on your left leg with your left knee slightly bent. Lift your right foot 2 to 6 inches (5 to 15 cm) off the ground and next to your left ankle (with your knee bent). Your arms are back, elbows are bent, and hands are by your hips (figure 5.10a).

2. Bend your left leg to a quarter-squat position as your shoulders and chest lean forward by bending at your waist. Explode up and forward, jumping off your left leg and driving both arms up and forward together (figure 5.10b). Drive your right knee up and forward while reaching with your foot as you hop forward for maximum height and distance.

3. Land under control on your right leg with a slightly bent knee (figure 5.10c). Now hop from the right leg to the left leg and continue this alternating hopping pattern for 8 to 10 repetitions.

Figure 5.10

Power Skip

1. Stand facing forward with your knees slightly bent, arms back, elbows bent, and hands by your hips.
2. Step forward and skip with your left foot (take off and land on the same foot) by driving your right knee and left arm forcefully up and forward as you leave the ground (figure 5.11). Drive your right arm back in an exaggerated running arm action.
3. Land on your slightly bent left leg and step forward on your right foot to repeat the skipping action for maximum height and distance.
4. Continue this skipping pattern for 8 to 10 repetitions.

Your arm action is a forceful exaggerated running motion with a hold at the top. Your knee drive is a forceful exaggerated up-and-forward motion. Your knee is also held at the top position. Upon landing, your opposite arm and knee are driven up and forward.

Figure 5.11

Bound

1. Stand facing forward with your knees slightly bent, arms back, elbows bent, and hands by your hips.
2. Bound up and forward off your left foot, drive your right knee up and forward in a forceful and exaggerated motion, and hold at the top position while in the air (figure 5.12). Drive both arms up and forward forcefully together and also hold at the top position. Your left leg hangs extended behind you. Before landing, your right knee and hands lower to prepare for the next bound off your right leg.
3. Landing on your slightly bent right leg, repeat the technique as you explosively bound up and forward in a continuous alternating pattern for 8 to 10 repetitions.

Figure 5.12

Bounds are defined by quick and explosive takeoff and landing transitions. Bounds build to maximum height and distance while suspended in the air at the top position for as long as possible with each bound.

BOX JUMPS

For safety, establish proper technique on lower boxes before progressing to higher boxes. Knee angles upon landing on the box must be a minimum of 90 degrees, preferably greater, or the box is too high for you.

DVD Single-Leg Spring-Up

Height of box: 12 to 24 inches (30 to 60 cm)

Number of boxes: 1

1. Stand sideways to the box with your right shoulder facing the box and your right foot on top of the box with a bent knee so that your leg (knee to ankle) is straight up and down (figure 5.13a). Your left foot is behind your right foot in alignment with your right hip next to the box (feet are hip-width apart). Your arms are back, elbows are bent, and hands are by your hips. Your weight is on your left leg with a slightly bent knee.

Figure 5.13

2. Transfer your weight to your right foot as you drive your arms forward and up. Jump straight up off your right leg as high as possible (figure 5.13b). Land on your right foot on top of the box and return to the starting position.

3. Repeat the same sequence under control for 6 to 8 repetitions. Turn around and repeat the spring-ups with your left leg.

Advanced version: Do the spring-ups with a touch-and-go sequence with your ground foot.

Caution: The starting knee angle on top of the box should not be less than 90 degrees.

Single-Leg Side-to-Side Box Jump

Height of box: 12 to 24 inches (30 to 60 cm)

Number of boxes: 1

1. Stand sideways to the box with your right shoulder facing the box and your right foot on top of the box with a bent knee so that your leg (knee to ankle) is straight up and down (figure 5.14a). Your left foot is behind your right foot in alignment with your right hip next to the box (feet are hip-width apart). Your arms are back, elbows are bent, and hands are by your hips. Your weight is on your left leg with a slightly bent knee.

2. Transfer your weight onto your right foot as you drive your arms forward and up and jump up off your right leg as high as possible while traveling laterally to the right in the air to the opposite side of the box (figure 5.14b).

3. Land on top of the box with your left foot and your left knee bent. Then your right foot lands on the ground on the opposite side of the box with a slightly bent knee (figure 5.14c).

4. Repeat the same technique, jumping off your left leg and returning to the starting position. Continue this sequence under control for 6 to 8 repetitions.

Advanced version: Do the Single-Leg Side-to-Side Jumps with a touch-and-go sequence with your ground foot.

Caution: The starting knee angle on top of the box should not be less than 90 degrees.

Figure 5.14

DVD **Alternating Power Jump**

Height of box: 12 to 24 inches (30 to 60 cm)

Number of boxes: 1

1. Stand facing the box with your right foot on the box and your right knee bent so that your leg (knee to ankle) is straight up and down (figure 5.15*a*). Your weight is on your left leg, which is on the ground with a slightly bent knee. Your feet are hip-width apart, arms are back, elbows are bent, and hands are by your hips.

2. Transfer your weight onto your right foot as you drive your arms forward and up and jump straight up off your right leg as high as possible (figure 5.15*b*). Alternate your legs in the air; your left foot lands first on top of the box and the knee is bent (figure 5.15*c*). Then your right foot lands on the ground in front of the box, and the knee is slightly bent.

3. Repeat the same technique, jumping off your left leg and returning to the starting position. Continue this alternating sequence under control for 6 to 8 repetitions.

Advanced version: Do the Alternating Power Jumps with touch-and-go jumping.

Caution: The starting knee angle on top of the box should not be less than 90 degrees.

Figure 5.15

Quick-Feet Plyometrics

Powerful movements are enhanced by speed. You can develop and improve the ability to quickly perform and repeat eccentric and concentric movements through a series of quick-feet plyometric exercises. Basketball movements that are improved by quick-feet plyometrics include a quick first step to get by a defender and quicker defensive reactions.

LINE DRILLS

The line drills use the sideline or baseline markings on a basketball court.

Double-Leg Forward and Back

1. Stand facing the line with your feet hip-width apart, knees slightly bent, and elbows bent approximately 90 degrees.

2. Jump back and forth over the line as quickly as possible, staying close to the floor. Continue this touch-and-go pattern for 10 jumps on each side of the line.

Single-Leg Forward and Back

1. Stand facing the line with your feet slightly less than hip-width apart. Stand on your right foot with your right knee slightly bent. Lift your left foot 2 to 6 inches (5 to 15 cm) off the ground and next to your right ankle (with your knee bent). Your arms are back, elbows are bent, and hands are by your hips.

2. Jump on your right foot back and forth over the line as quickly as possible, staying close to the floor.

3. Continue this touch-and-go pattern for 10 jumps on each side of the line. Repeat with your left foot.

Double-Leg Side-to-Side

DVD

1. Stand sideways to the line with your right shoulder facing the line. Your feet are slightly closer than hip width, knees are slightly bent, and elbows are bent approximately 90 degrees.

2. Jump sideways over the line as quickly as possible, staying close to the floor.

3. Continue this touch-and-go pattern for 10 jumps on each side of the line.

ⒹⓋⒹ Single-Leg Side-to-Side

1. Stand sideways to the line with your right shoulder facing the line. Your feet are slightly less than shoulder-width apart while you stand on your right foot with your right knee slightly bent. Lift your left foot 2 to 6 inches (5 to 15 cm) off the ground and next to your right ankle (with your knee bent). Your arms are back, elbows are bent, and hands are by your hips.

2. Jump on your right foot side to side over the line as quickly as possible, staying close to the floor.

3. Continue this touch-and-go pattern for 10 jumps on each side of the line. Repeat with your left foot.

Double-Leg Diagonal

1. Stand sideways to the line with your right shoulder facing the line and your feet slightly closer than hip-width apart, knees slightly bent, arms back, elbows bent approximately 90 degrees.

2. Jump forward diagonally back and forth over the line with consecutive 45-degree angled jumps, staying close to the floor and approximately 6 inches on each side of the line.

3. Continue these diagonal jumps as quickly as possible as you travel forward down the line for 10 jumps on each side of the line.

ⒹⓋⒹ Single-Leg Diagonal

1. Stand sideways to the line with your right shoulder facing the line. Your feet are slightly less than hip-width apart while you stand on your right foot with your right knee slightly bent. Lift your left foot 2 to 6 inches (5 to 15 cm) off the ground and next to your right ankle (with your knee bent). Your arms are back, elbows are bent, and hands are by your hips.

2. Jump forward over the line with consecutive 45-degree angled jumps on your right foot, staying close to the floor.

3. Continue these diagonal jumps as quickly as possible as you travel forward down the line for 10 jumps on each side of the line. Repeat with your left foot.

BOX DRILLS

Quick-Step Box Touch

Height of box: 4 to 12 inches (10 to 30 cm)

Number of boxes: 1

1. Stand facing the box with a slight forward lean of your shoulders. Your feet are hip-width apart, knees are slightly bent, arms are back, elbows are bent, and hands are by your hips (figure 5.16a).

2. With your right foot, step up onto the box as fast as possible (figure 5.16b). As soon as your right foot touches the box, immediately step onto the box with your left foot (figure 5.16c). As soon as your left foot touches the box, immediately step back down to the ground with your right foot to the original starting position (figure 5.16d). As soon as your right foot touches the ground, your left foot returns to the original starting position from the top of the box (figure 5.16e). Once the left foot touches the ground, the right foot starts the sequence again.

Figure 5.16

Figure 5.16

3. Repeat for as many repetitions as possible in a 10- to 30-second time period. Your arms should move in a running arm action with a limited range of motion. Two options that might help you with the proper exercise tempo and rhythm are a cadence of 1, 2, 3, 4 (right, left, right, left) or up, up, down, down (right, left, right, left).

Lateral Box Shuffle

Height of box: 4 to 12 inches (10 to 30 cm)

Number of boxes: 1

1. Stand sideways next to the box with your right shoulder facing the box and a slight forward lean of your shoulders. Your feet are hip-width apart, knees are slightly bent, arms are back, elbows are bent, and hands are by your hips (figure 5.17a).

2. With your right foot, step laterally to the right up onto the far middle of the box as fast as possible (figure 5.17b). As soon as your right foot touches the box, immediately step up onto the near middle of the box with your left foot (figure 5.17c). As soon as your left foot touches the box, immediately step down to the ground on the opposite side of the box with your right foot, leaving enough room

Figure 5.17

for your left foot (figure 5.17*d*). As soon as your right foot touches the ground, your left foot follows (figure 5.17*e*). As soon as your left foot touches the ground, immediately step back onto the far middle of the box with your left foot. As soon as your left foot touches the box, immediately step up onto the near middle of the box with your right foot. As soon as your right foot touches the box, your left foot returns to the original starting position and your right foot follows.

3. As soon as your right foot touches the ground, repeat the same sequence for as many repetitions as possible in a 10- to 30-second time period. You can move your arms in a running arm action with a limited range of motion or maintain the arm position used in the original starting position. Two options that might help you with the proper exercise tempo and rhythm are a cadence of 1, 2, 3, 4 (right, left, right, left) or up, up, down, down (right, left, right, left).

Figure 5.17

Upper-Body Plyometrics

Upper-body plyometrics train the chest, back, torso, and arms for powerful, quick, and explosive movements. The following exercises will help improve shooting range and passing speed and distance.

PUSH-UPS

Push-Up With a Clap

1. Your hands are on the ground shoulder-width apart, and your arms are straight. Your body is in a straight fixed position with your toes touching the ground (figure 5.18a).

2. Bend your arms and lower your body until your chest comes within 1 inch (2.5 cm) of the ground. Explosively push up so that your hands leave the ground, and clap your hands together at the highest point off the ground (figure 5.18b).

Figure 5.18

3. Land in the starting position with slightly bent elbows and repeat for up to 10 repetitions.

Push-Up With a Platform

Height of platform: 2 to 18 inches (5 to 45 cm)

Platforms may include boxes, bumper plates, and mats placed just outside the hands.

1. Your hands are on the ground shoulder-width apart, and your arms are straight. Your body is in a straight fixed position with your toes touching the ground (figure 5.19a).

Figure 5.19

2. Bend your arms and lower your body until your chest comes within 1 inch (2.5 cm) of the ground (figure 5.19b). Explosively push up so that your hands leave the ground (figure 5.19c) and land on each platform with slightly bent elbows.

3. Bend your arms and lower your body until you reach a slightly stretched position through your chest and shoulders. Then push up and lower your hands one at a time to the original starting position.

4. Repeat for up to 10 repetitions.

Figure 5.19

MEDICINE BALL PLYOMETRIC DRILLS

For the purpose of these drills, try to use a rubber inflatable medicine ball that bounces. Suggested medicine ball weight progressions are 2, 4, 6, 8, 10, and 15 pounds (approximately 1, 2, 3, 4, 5, 7 kg).

Medicine Ball Chest Pass

1. Stand 8 to 16 feet (2.4 to 4.8 m) away from and facing your partner or the wall. Feet are shoulder-width apart and knees are slightly bent. Hold the medicine ball with both hands at your chest, elbows bent.

2. Step forward and perform a two-hand chest pass to your partner or off the wall at chest height (figure 5.20). Catch the ball from your partner or off the wall with your arms extended. Quickly recoil, touching the ball to your chest, and explosively repeat the chest pass for 10 repetitions.

Figure 5.20

DVD ## Medicine Ball Overhead Pass

1. Stand 10 to 20 feet (3 to 6 m) away from and facing your partner or the wall. Feet are shoulder-width apart and knees are slightly bent. Hold the medicine ball with both hands overhead, elbows bent.

2. Bring the ball slightly forward before moving it back behind your head with your elbows bent at 90 degrees and your upper body arched slightly back. Step forward and extend your arms while performing an overhead pass to your partner or the wall (figure 5.21). On the follow-through, the arms and upper body move forward with the release of the ball.

Figure 5.21

3. Catch the ball from your partner or off the wall with your arms extended. Quickly recoil, bringing the ball over your head, and explosively repeat the overhead pass for 10 repetitions.

Medicine Ball Side Pass

1. Stand 8 to 16 feet (2.4 to 4.8 m) away from and facing your partner or the wall. Your feet are shoulder-width apart and knees are slightly bent. Hold the medicine ball in front of you with both hands behind the ball, palms facing forward, and arms straight.

2. Bend your knees, rotate to your right a quarter turn (your left shoulder will be facing forward). Your arms are straight and your right hand is on the top of the ball and your left hand is below with your palms facing forward (figure 5.22).

3. From this coiled position, rotate forward with an explosive release of the ball to your partner's left side or to the wall with a straight-ahead pass.

Figure 5.22

4. The catching position is the same as the release position. Catch the ball from your partner or off the wall, recoil a quarter turn under control, and repeat the pass.

5. Continue this technique for 10 side passes and then repeat the 10 passes on the opposite side.

Advanced version: With a partner, pass and catch to the same shoulder (right shoulder to right shoulder). This diagonal pass requires a fuller rotation.

Medicine Ball Drop

DVD

1. Lie on your back on a flat dumbbell bench with both arms extended straight up and your hands ready to catch the ball. Your partner stands at the head end of the bench with the medicine ball extended over your hands (figure 5.23*a*).
2. Your partner drops the ball into your hands. Catch the ball, quickly touch the ball to your chest (figure 5.23*b*), and explosively pass the ball straight up for maximum height (figure 5.23*c*). Your partner catches the ball.
3. Repeat for 8 to 10 passes.

Advanced version: Your partner stands on an elevated platform.

Figure 5.23

Plyometrics With a Basketball

Depending on his or her position and minutes, a basketball player will jump an average of 75 to 120 times per game. Approximately two-thirds of the jumps are made with two legs, and one-third are single-leg jumps. Although the majority of jumps in a game are double leg, it is necessary to train each leg equally. Training both single- and double-leg jumps develops strength, power, and proper muscle balance. It also minimizes the risk of injury to weaker, less developed muscles. The following drills use plyometric training with basketball-specific movements.

Double-Leg Jump Hook

Two people are needed for this drill: the passer and shooter/rebounder. One basketball is also needed.

1. The shooter/rebounder stands on the left low block with his or her back to the basket and feet shoulder-width apart. Knees are slightly bent and hands are ready to catch different types of passes. The passer is on the left side of the court holding a basketball.

2. The passer performs a post entry pass from various positions on the left side of the court. The shooter/rebounder catches the ball, takes a step toward the middle of the lane with the left foot, and brings the right foot toward the left foot. The shooter/rebounder explosively jumps off both feet and shoots a jump hook with the right hand. The shooter/rebounder rebounds the ball and passes it back to the passer. Then the shooter/rebounder returns to the starting position on the same block or runs to the other block and repeats the sequence, using the opposite right–left footwork and shooting a jump hook with the left hand.

3. The shooter/rebounder performs 3 to 5 jump hooks on each block.

Advanced version: Do the jump hook after 1 dribble.

Single-Leg Running Hook

Two people are needed for this drill: the passer and shooter/rebounder. One basketball is also needed.

1. The shooter/rebounder stands on the left low block with his or her back to the basket and feet shoulder-width apart. Knees are slightly bent, and hands are ready to catch different types of passes. The passer is on the left side of the court holding a basketball.

2. The passer performs a post entry pass from various positions on the left side of the court. The shooter/rebounder catches the ball and takes a step toward the middle of the lane with the left foot. The shooter/rebounder explosively jumps off the left leg while shooting a right-hand hook shot. The shooter/rebounder rebounds the ball and passes it back to the passer. Then the shooter/rebounder returns to the starting position on the same block or runs to the other block and repeats the sequence, using the right leg and a left-hand hook shot.

3. The shooter/rebounder performs 3 to 5 running hooks from each block.

Advanced version: Do the running hook after 1 dribble.

Double-Leg Power Dunk or Layup

Two people are needed for this drill: the shooter and rebounder/ball replacer. Two basketballs are needed. Start with one basketball on each low block.

1. The shooter stands under the basket, facing the court. Feet are shoulder-width apart and knees are slightly bent. The rebounder/ball replacer is in the lane in front of and facing the basket.

2. The shooter picks up a ball as fast as possible, then performs a drop step and jumps explosively as high as possible off both legs for a dunk or layup. The shooter then immediately runs to the other ball and repeats.

3. The shooter alternates from one block to the other block for 3 to 5 dunks or layups on each side. After each shot, the rebounder/ball replacer immediately rebounds the ball and replaces it on the block.

Single-Leg Power Dunk or Layup

Two people are needed for this drill: the passer/rebounder and shooter. One basketball is also needed.

1. The shooter stands on the right corner of the free-throw line and lane (the right elbow), facing the basket. The passer/rebounder is in the lane in front of the basket, holding the ball and facing the basket.

2. The shooter starts toward the basket, receives a bounce pass from the passer, and, without dribbling, jumps explosively as high as possible off of the left leg, dunking the ball or laying it up with the right hand. The shooter immediately runs to the left elbow as the passer rebounds the ball. The shooter turns and runs to the basket to receive a bounce pass for a left-hand dunk or layup while jumping explosively off the right leg.

3. Continue this drill for 3 to 5 dunks or layups on each side.

Make sure to count the total number of foot contacts in each workout and stay within your category (beginning, intermediate, or advanced).

Chapter 6

Speed

Speed is another component that separates athletes and can be a big advantage on the basketball court. Most people believe that a person is either born with speed or born without it. Although that is true to an extent, most athletes, no matter what their size or genetic makeup, can improve their running speed. Only a few athletes have world-class speed. Slow runners may not become fast, but they can become faster.

Speed is the time it takes to move from point A to point B. Acceleration speed is the rate of change in velocity, which allows an athlete to reach maximum speed in a minimum time. When relating this to the game of basketball, speed must be developed not only straight ahead but also in other movement patterns that mimic the game. Many of the same principles involved in sprinting straight ahead apply to other movements—lateral, backward, and all different angles.

FUNDAMENTALS OF SPEED

Stride frequency combined with stride length equals running speed. Stride frequency is the number of strides in a given time or distance. Stride length is the distance covered in one stride during running.

Stride frequency is more difficult to train partly because of genetic limitations. With proper strength, reactive neuromuscular efficiency, and overspeed training techniques, stride frequency can increase. Stride length is a highly trainable component for improving speed, contrary to stride frequency, making it the easiest way of improving speed and acceleration.

PROPER BODY POSITION AND ALIGNMENT

Proper sprint mechanics allow for maximum muscle force to be generated so that maximum velocity can be achieved in the shortest possible time. The three main components of proper running mechanics are body alignment, arm action, and leg action.

Proper body alignment allows for the most efficient application of force. Any deviation from the proper body alignment will negatively affect the application of force. The following are guidelines for proper body position and alignment:

- The ears, shoulders, hips, knees, and ankles should be in a straight line. Maintain this position when sprinting.
- The eyes should focus straight ahead. Avoid head movement up, down, or side to side.
- The shoulders should be squared and relaxed, with no torso rotation.
- The elbows should be fixed at a 90-degree angle and close to the body, swinging in a straight line.
- The hands should be slightly open in loose fists and should go no higher than the shoulders on the forward swing. On the back swing, the hands are driven down, back, and through the hips.
- The knee of the drive leg is driven forward, not upward, in a straight line. The push leg is fully extended.

DEVELOPMENTAL SPEED DRILLS

These drills emphasize actual sprint technique, but the principles also apply to other movements, such as defensive shuffling, backpedaling, and many combinations of movements that basketball players use during practices and games.

© NBAE/Getty Images

Swin Cash of the Detroit Shock dribbles ahead of Ticha Penicheiro of the Sacramento Monarchs during the 2006 WNBA Finals. Good speed makes it possible for a player to outrun a defender and get the ball to the offensive end.

Beginning Drills

The beginning drills focus on arm action and knee drive with bent arms and legs and straight arms and legs. The first two drills focus specifically on arm action and knee drive. The third drill, High Knee March, uses both arm action and knee drive. The Drum Major March focuses on higher (exaggerated) straight arm and leg actions.

BEGINNING SPEED DEVELOPMENT EXERCISES

Arm Action

1. Stand with your feet hip-width apart or with one foot slightly forward in a staggered position with slightly bent knees. Your elbows are flexed at a 90-degree angle and at your sides. Your hands are in loose fists.

2. Your arms act as a pendulum, swinging in a straight line with your shoulders as the pivot points. One arm is driven forward and up to shoulder height while the other arm is driven down, back, and through your hip (figure 6.1).

3. Perform this alternating arm movement with powerful movements. Do 30 to 60 repetitions with each arm.

Figure 6.1

Knee Drive

1. Stand with your feet shoulder-width apart and knees slightly bent. Lean forward slightly at the waist. Your arms are fully extended in front with your hands on a waist-high support such as a wall, bar, table, or weight machine.

2. Drive one knee forward and up while keeping your body square to the support (figure 6.2). Immediately drive your foot back to the starting position. This is a rapid knee drive and hip extension floor tap drill.

3. Do 10 repetitions then switch legs and repeat.

Figure 6.2

High Knee March

1. Stand with your feet shoulder-width apart, arms straight, and hands at your sides.

2. March forward, driving your knees as high as possible with each step (figure 6.3). Your arm action is the same technique as the Arm Action drill.

3. March for 10 to 20 repetitions with each leg.

Figure 6.3

Drum Major March

1. Stand with your feet shoulder-width apart, arms straight, and hands at your sides.

2. March forward, keeping your arms and legs straight with a high (exaggerated) alternating leg and arm action (figure 6.4). Your lift leg should be straight until it's above your waist and then slightly bent when contacting the ground with the ball of your foot. Your standing leg should be slightly bent.

3. March for 10 to 20 repetitions with each leg.

Figure 6.4

Intermediate Drills

The intermediate drills focus on faster movements that use both arm and leg actions. The Butt Kicks focus on the heel-to-butt action with no forward leg drive. The second and third drills are faster and more dynamic versions of the third and fourth beginning drills. The High Knee Skip uses a unique arm and leg action with a skipping rhythm.

INTERMEDIATE SPEED DEVELOPMENT EXERCISES

Butt Kicks

1. Stand with your feet shoulder-width apart. Lean forward slightly at your waist. Arms are straight and hands are at your sides.
2. While moving forward, keep your thighs almost perpendicular to the ground (not moving your knees forward) and try to kick your butt with your heels using an alternating leg action (figure 6.5). Your arm action is the same technique as in the Arm Action drill but not as forceful.
3. Perform this drill to half court or the full length of the court.

Figure 6.5

High Knee Run

1. Stand with your feet shoulder-width apart, arms straight, and hands at your sides.
2. While running forward, drive your knees up as high as possible (figure 6.6). Your arm action is the same technique as in the Arm Action drill. This is a fast-tempo, rhythmic drill with shortened quick strides.
3. Perform this drill to half court or the full length of the court.

Figure 6.6

Drum Major Run

1. Stand with your feet shoulder-width apart, arms straight, and hands at your sides.
2. While running forward, keep your arms and legs straight with a high (exaggerated) alternating leg and arm action (figure 6.7). Your lift leg should be straight until it's above your waist and then slightly bent when contacting the ground with the ball of your foot. Your standing leg should be slightly bent.
3. Run for 10 to 20 repetitions with each leg or the full length of the court.

Figure 6.7

High Knee Skips

1. Stand with your feet shoulder-width apart, arms straight, and hands at your sides.
2. Step forward and skip with your left foot (take off and land on the same foot) by driving your right knee up as high as possible and left arm up and forward (figure 6.8). Drive your right arm back using proper arm action while keeping your left foot close to the ground.
3. Landing on your slightly bent left leg, step forward on your right foot to repeat the skipping action. This is a fast-tempo, rhythmic skip.
4. Perform this drill to half court or the full length of the court.

Figure 6.8

Advanced Speed Drills

Advanced speed drills involve resistance and assistance overspeed training. Resistance speed training can be performed while running up hills, stairs, and bleachers or while using equipment for the resistance. Equipment used for resistance speed training includes running harnesses and belts, resistance tubing, sleds, parachutes, weighted vests, and swimming pools.

Assistance overspeed training drills allow you to run faster than you can on your own. Assistance overspeed training involves sprinting on a slight downhill slope (never more than 6 percent grade), using prestretched tubing, being towed, or sprinting on an overspeed treadmill. For safety reasons, we do not recommend being towed or sprinting on an overspeed treadmill.

Resistance Speed Drills

The resistance speed drills include incline running drills and equipment resistance running drills. The incline running drills are uphill sprints and strides or stairs and bleachers. The equipment resistance drills are acceleration drills that use harnesses (belts or tubing), running sleds, parachutes, or weighted vests or are performed in a swimming pool.

INCLINE RUNNING DRILLS

Uphill Sprints and Strides

Distance: 30 to 120 yards (27 to 109 m)

Incline angles: May vary from moderate to steep; the steeper the incline, the shorter the distance of the run

1. Stand with your feet in a staggered position with your knees slightly bent. Lean forward slightly at the waist. Elbows are flexed at a 90-degree angle and are at your sides. One hand is in front of your shoulder and the other hand is next to and slightly behind your hip.

2. Drive your arms and knees forward and up in a powerful and forceful action as you stride or sprint up the hill. Longer distances are strides and shorter distances are sprints. Strides are three-quarter speed and sprints are all-out efforts. Use proper running technique.

Stairs

Stair variables: Football and track stadiums or basketball gyms with long, straight stairways

Distance: 20 to 120 stair steps

Quick Step

1. Stand with your feet in a staggered position with your knees slightly bent. Lean forward slightly at the waist. Elbows are flexed at a 90-degree angle and are at your sides. One hand is in front of your shoulder and the other hand is next to and slightly behind your hip.

2. Land on every step as quickly as possible using a shortened running motion and staying on the balls of your feet.

3. Range: 20 to 100 stair steps.

Two Steps

1. Stand with your feet in a staggered position with your knees slightly bent. Lean forward slightly at the waist. Elbows are flexed at a 90-degree angle and are at your sides. One hand is in front of your shoulder and the other hand is next to and slightly behind your hip.

2. Land on every second step as quickly as possible using a fast running motion. Drive your arms and knees forward and up in a powerful and forceful action as you stride or sprint up the stairs.

3. Longer distances are strides and shorter distances are sprints. Use proper running technique.

4. Range: 40 to 100 stair steps.

Three Steps

1. Stand with your feet in a staggered position and your knees slightly bent. Lean forward slightly at the waist. Elbows are flexed at a 90-degree angle and are at your sides. One hand is in front of your shoulder and the other hand is next to and slightly behind your hip.

2. Land on every third step as quickly as possible using a fast running motion. Drive your arms and knees forward and up in a powerful and forceful action as you stride or sprint up the stairs.

3. Longer distances are strides and shorter distances are sprints. Use proper running technique.

4. Range: 60 to 120 stair steps.

Caution: Stair heights and depths vary. For safety reasons, be careful with foot placements on each stair step.

Bleachers

Bleacher variables: Football or track stadiums

Distance: 40 to 100 bleachers

Quick Stride

1. Stand with your feet in a staggered position and your knees slightly bent. Lean forward slightly at the waist. Elbows are flexed at a 90-degree angle and are at your sides. One hand is in front of your shoulder and the other hand is next to and slightly behind your hip.

2. Land on every bleacher as quickly as possible using a shortened running motion and staying on the balls of your feet. Drive your arms and knees forward and up in a powerful and forceful action as you stride or sprint up the bleachers.

3. Longer distances are strides and shorter distances are sprints. Use proper running technique.

4. Range : 40 to 100 bleachers.

Double-Bleacher Stride

1. Stand with your feet in a staggered position and your knees slightly bent. Lean forward slightly at the waist. Elbows are flexed at a 90-degree angle and are at your sides. One hand is in front of your shoulder and the other hand is next to and slightly behind your hip.
2. Land on every second bleacher as quickly as possible using a fast running motion. Drive your arms and knees forward and up in a powerful and forceful action as you stride or sprint up the bleachers.
3. Longer distances are strides and shorter distances are sprints. Use proper running technique. Do double bleachers as far as you can, then switch to single to the finish line if necessary.
4. Range: 40 to 100 bleachers.

Caution: Run on the bleachers above the supports.

EQUIPMENT RESISTANCE DRILLS

Equipment needed: Harnesses, belts, tubing, sleds, parachutes, weighted vests, and flotation vests

Acceleration Drill With a Harness, Belt, or Tubing

Location: Basketball court, track, or field

Distance: 10 to 30 yards (30 yards is approximately the length of a basketball court)

These drills require 2 people; partner 1 is the lead partner running against the resistance of partner 2, the trailing partner. Partner 1 wears the belt around the waist or the harness around the shoulders and waist. Partner 2 holds on to the handles at the end of the rope or tubing, which is attached to the belt or harness. The rope or tubing needs to be held tight without slack at the start and throughout the drill.

1. Partner 1 stands with the feet staggered and knees slightly bent while leaning slightly forward at the waist. Elbows are flexed at a 90-degree angle and are at the sides. One hand is in front of the shoulder and the other hand is next to and slightly behind the hip. Partner 2 stands with the feet staggered and knees slightly bent and is leaning slightly backward.
2. Partner 1 drives the arms and knees forward and up in a powerful and forceful action while sprinting to the finish line. Partner 2 controls the speed of the drill with the pace of his resistance trailing jog (figure 6.9).

Figure 6.9

Note: If you are training with another athlete, you can switch positions after each sprint.

Tubing differences: With tubing, partner 1 sprints until the tubing is stretched before partner 2 starts to trail.

Fixed tubing: Partner 1 sprints until the tubing is stretched and then sprints in place for 10 to 30 repetitions before carefully returning to the starting position.

Acceleration Drill With a Running Sled

Location: Grass or Astroturf field

Distance: 20 to 60 yards

Put on the harness or belt that is connected to the sled and walk forward until the rope is tight without slack. Start with lighter weights on the sled before advancing to heavier weights.

1. Stand with your feet in a staggered position and your knees slightly bent. Lean forward slightly at the waist. Elbows are flexed at a 90-degree angle and are at your sides. One hand is in front of your shoulder and the other hand is next to and slightly behind your hip.

2. Drive your arms and knees forward and up in a powerful and forceful action as you sprint down the field. After running through the finish line, slowly decelerate under control. Use proper running technique.

Caution: Warm up with strides before doing sled running.

Parachute Sprint

Location: Basketball court, track, or field

Distance: 30 to 100 yards (30 yards is approximately the length of a basketball court)

Put on the harness or belt that is connected to the parachute and loosen up the parachute so it is free and open with untangled strings to start. Walk forward so the parachute is straight behind you.

1. Stand with your feet in a staggered position and your knees slightly bent. Lean forward slightly at the waist. Elbows are flexed at a 90-degree angle and are at your sides. One hand is in front of your shoulder and the other hand is next to and slightly behind your hip.
2. Drive your arms and knees forward and up in a powerful and forceful action as you sprint down the court, track, or field using proper running technique.

Caution: Warm up with strides before doing parachute sprints.

Weighted-Vest Sprint

Location: Basketball court, track, or field

Distance: 30 to 60 yards

We recommend the jacket-type weighted vests that are secured tightly to your body with adjustable straps or zippers. Start with lighter weights in the vest before advancing to heavier weights.

1. Stand with your feet in a staggered position and your knees slightly bent. Lean forward slightly at the waist. Elbows are flexed at a 90-degree angle and are at your sides. One hand is in front of your shoulder and the other hand is next to and slightly behind your hip.
2. Drive your arms and knees forward and up in a powerful and forceful action as you sprint down the court, track, or field using proper running technique.

Caution: Warm up with strides before doing weighted-vest sprints.

Water Resistance Drills

Location: Swimming pool, therapy pool, river, lake, or ocean

Equipment: Basketball, running, or swimming shoes; flotation vest or belt; or wall tether

Exercise time: 10 to 60 seconds

Water resistance drills are all-out sprint intervals with proper running technique, regardless of which of the five variables you choose to work with: water depth, with or without a flotation device, in place or traveling, tethered to a wall while wearing a belt, or water current. It is not necessary to be able to swim to do these drills.

Water depth: Two different water depths are recommended for the water resistance drills: shoulder to neck high (feet touch bottom) and over your head (head stays above water):

1. Touch the bottom, standing straight up in water that is shoulder to neck high.
2. Touch the bottom to make sure the water is over your head when you stand straight. Your head stays above the water as you perform the drills.

With or without a flotation device: You may choose to wear a secured flotation vest for buoyancy and safety. Not wearing a flotation vest makes the water resistance drills harder.

In place or traveling: The in-place sprinting action is more upright and does not travel. The traveling sprinting action has a forward lean and movement.

Tethered to a wall while wearing a belt: This in-place action has a forward lean. You sprint away from the wall tether.

Water current: This action has a forward lean and movement. You sprint into the water current.

Note: Your head is above the water for all water resistance drills.

Assistance Overspeed Drills

The two assistance overspeed drills that we recommend are downhill sprinting and sprinting with prestretched tubing. These are the safest of the overspeed drills.

ASSISTANCE OVERSPEED EXERCISES

Downhill Sprint

Downhill sprinting is done on a slope at 6 percent grade or less. Do not downhill sprint on a steeper slope.

Location: A safe running surface (grass, sand, track, turf, or pavement) with an appropriate length to allow you to slow down under control (20 yards past the finish)

Sprinting distance: 20 to 60 yards (18 to 55 m)

1. Stand with your feet in a staggered position and your knees slightly bent. Lean forward slightly at the waist. Elbows are flexed at a 90-degree angle and are at your sides. One hand is in front of your shoulder and the other hand is next to and slightly behind your hip.
2. Drive your arms and knees forward in a powerful and forceful action as you sprint down the hill using faster but proper running technique.
3. After sprinting through the finish line, decelerate under control.

Caution: Warm up with strides before doing downhill sprinting.

Prestretched Tubing Sprint

The prestretched tubing is fixed at one end (attached to an immovable object or held by a partner) and secured to the sprinter by a harness or belt.

Location: Basketball court, track, or field

Distance: 20 to 40 yards (18 to 37 m), depending on the length and thickness of the tubing

Put on the harness or belt that is connected to the tubing and backpedal to a sufficient tubing stretch for the desired resistance and distance.

1. Stand with your feet in a staggered position and your knees slightly bent. Lean forward slightly at the waist. Elbows are flexed at a 90-degree angle and are at your sides. One hand is in front of your shoulder and the other hand is next to and slightly behind your hip.
2. Sprint toward the fixed end of the tubing using faster but proper running technique. Sprint until the stretch is out of the tubing and you are through the finish line.
3. Decelerate under control.

Caution: Warm up with strides before sprinting with prestretched tubing. Stay away from the fixed end of the tubing during the finish.

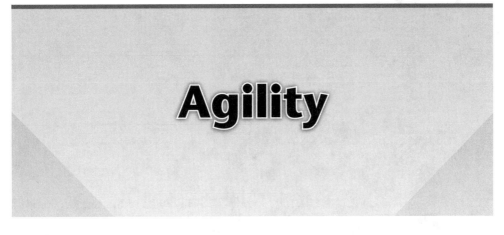

Chapter 7

Agility

Basketball is a game of movement. A player blocks a shot, rebounds the ball, and sends an outlet pass to a teammate, leading to a fast break. Using a sprint dribble, the player explores and reacts to the defense as his teammates fill the lanes looking to score. Successful basketball players have developed the art of changing direction while performing at a fast pace and high skill level. The ability to control one's body while performing basketball skills at a high speed demonstrates great agility. Agility is the ability to change body direction quickly, explosively, and under control.

At each successive level of competition—middle school, high school, college, and professional—agility becomes more important, both on the offensive and defensive ends. As a defender, your ability to keep an offensive player in front of you plays a big role in how successful you will be. Also, as an offensive player, your ability to get past a defender will help create plays not only for yourself but for your teammates as well. Just being quick or fast is only half the battle. You must perform basketball movements and skills under control at all times, which will make you a more efficient player.

When you train to improve your ability to move more quickly, explosively, and efficiently, balance and coordination become very important. You must improve your ability to move on and off the court with agility training. You perform these skills each time you play the game; you change directions, accelerate, and decelerate while staying under control. While playing basketball, you experience unpredictable movement patterns. You must react to the game on the fly; for each higher level of play, this happens even faster.

Ray Allen of the Seattle Sonics sets up against Marquis Daniels of the Indiana Pacers. A player with good agility is better able to work around defenders, change directions quickly, and get the ball to teammates or the basket.

© Getty Images

DEVELOPING AGILITY

To improve agility, you must perform quality repetitions of a variety of agility drills that mimic the movements required during the game. Agility drills train the body to react more quickly and under control. By performing drills repeatedly in a practice setting, you become better when the skill is needed during the game. Just as shooting jump shots and free throws will help you become a better shooter, practicing agility drills will help you improve agility, thereby making you a better, more efficient all-around player.

By practicing agility movements, you will learn to cut down on the wasted motions that cause fatigue faster. And by learning to do the drills correctly and under control, you will learn to move more efficiently.

Because of individual physical differences, agility movements and technique are described only in general terms. Players move through a number of horizontal and vertical planes and must perform a variety of unpredictable movements rapidly. Agility involves acceleration, deceleration, and change of direction while moving at a fast speed and under control. The development of these components involves speed, power, quickness, and balance.

Basketball agility requires you to move rapidly and under control. You must train other components—flexibility, strength, speed, power, and balance—because these components contribute to improved agility.

YEARLY TRAINING SCHEDULE

Agility training should play a major role in a yearly conditioning program.

Off-season: During the off-season, players should make their greatest gains because they have more time to train. The off-season is the time to learn new drills and develop proper technique for all drills. Entire workouts can be devoted to agility training. Agility training should be done 2 or 3 days a week.

Preseason: Agility training continues, but the workouts are shorter and the work gets sharper. Agility workouts should be once or twice a week, depending on the needs of individual players.

In-season: Agility training is limited to a few drills that may be done as part of the daily dynamic warm-up. Players who do not play many minutes can continue agility training throughout the season. The amount depends on the needs of individual players.

GUIDELINES FOR AGILITY

Agility training requires proper footwear (basketball shoes) for agility drills. Drills should be done on a nonslip surface, such as a clean gym floor.

Perform drills at slow speeds first, beginning with proper technique and footwork. When you can perform repetitions successfully and under control, you can increase speed.

For every agility drill, start in the ready position: feet shoulder-width apart; ankles, knees, and hips flexed in a quarter-squat position; head and shoulders slightly forward with hips and ankles in a straight line. Keep knees and hips flexed and your center of gravity over the feet. The body cannot move quickly when it is standing straight up. From this position, you are ready to move in any direction and can hold this position if bumped from any angle. This ready position is the most efficient position for moving and reacting.

Agility drills should be short in duration (anaerobic), approximately 10 to 20 seconds. Each workout should include a variety of drills that involve multiple changes of directions as well as sprints, backpedals, shuffles, hops, skips, turns, rotations, and jumps. Workouts should start with a good warm-up and flexibility program (see chapter 2) and finish with a cool-down.

AGILITY DRILLS

The following 20 agility drills are separated into 7 categories: Hexagon, Ladder, Hurdle, Snake, Lane, Extended-Lane, and Full-Court drills.

The hexagon drill and ladder drills are not true agility drills; they are quick-feet drills. In the context of this book, however, they fit best with the agility drills.

HEXAGON DRILL

Hexagon

Setup: Use floor tape to mark a hexagon on the floor. Each of the 6 sides is 24 inches (60 cm) long.

1. Start in the ready position in the middle of the hexagon, facing the number 1 tape. Face that direction throughout the drill.

2. Jump with 2 feet over the number 1 tape and back to the middle of the hexagon (figure 7.1). Then jump at an angle over the number 2 tape and back to the middle. Continue this clockwise pattern for all 6 sides.

3. Repeat the drill in a counterclockwise direction.

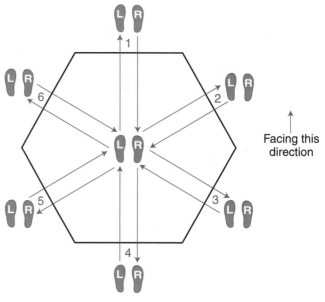

Figure 7.1

LADDER DRILLS

The quick-feet ladder is very versatile. With a little creativity, you can come up with many drills. Movement directions for the drills should include forward, backward, lateral, and angled. Movements include quick steps, hops, and jumps with 1 or 2 feet. Start with basic movements—running through the ladder 1 foot per square and 2 feet per square, lateral movements, and 1- and 2-foot hops and jumps. The following drills are more advanced.

Setup: Use a quick-feet ladder or use floor tape to make a ladder on the floor. For most quick-feet ladders that have 20 squares, each square is 16 to 20 inches (about 40 to 50 cm) wide and 16 to 18 inches (about 40 to 45 cm) long.

Hip Rotation

1. Start in the ready position at the near end of the ladder with the left foot outside the ladder to the left and the right foot in the first square (figure 7.2).

2. Hop in the air, rotating your hips 45 degrees to the right, keeping your head and shoulders square. Land with your right foot in the first square and your left foot in the second square.

3. Immediately after landing, quickly hop in the air. Land with your left foot in the second square and your right foot outside the second square to the right, facing straight ahead.

4. Immediately after landing, quickly hop in the air, rotating your hips 45 degrees to the left, keeping your head and shoulders square. Land with your left foot in the second square and your right foot in the third square.

5. Immediately after landing, quickly hop in the air, landing with your right foot in the third square and your left foot outside the third square to the left, facing straight ahead.

6. Continue this "straight, right rotation, straight, left rotation, straight" sequence for the length of the ladder.

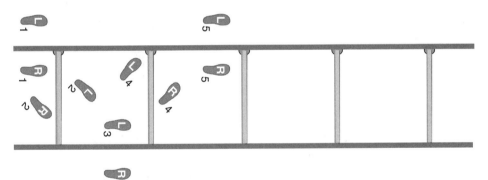

Figure 7.2

DVD **Skier**

1. Start in the ready position at the near end of the ladder with the left foot outside the ladder to the left and the right foot in the first square (figure 7.3).
2. Hop in the air and land with your right foot outside to the right of the first square and your left foot in the middle of the second square.
3. Immediately hop in the air and land with your left foot outside to the left of the second square and your right foot in the middle of the third square.
4. Continue this "right foot out, left foot in and left foot out, right foot in" sequence for the length of the ladder. Your head, shoulders, hips, and feet all stay facing straight up the ladder.

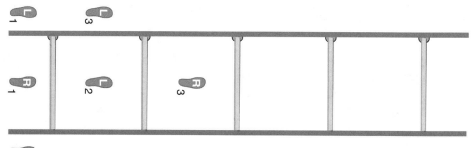

Figure 7.3

DVD **Icky Shuffle**

1. Start in the ready position at the near end of the ladder with both feet on the left side of the ladder.
2. Begin by stepping into the first square with your right foot. Quickly follow with your left foot, stepping into the same square.
3. Once your left foot touches, immediately step with your right foot outside the ladder to the right. Once your right foot touches, quickly step with your left foot into the second square.
4. Follow with your right foot into the same square and immediately step with your left foot outside the ladder to the left.
5. Continue this "in, in, out" sequence the length of the ladder.

Advanced version, Reactive Icky Shuffle: In this drill, the footwork is the same as the icky shuffle, except on a coach's or partner's clap, change direction. As you move forward, when you hear the first clap, immediately reverse direction and move backward using the same footwork. When you hear the second clap, immediately reverse direction and move forward using the same footwork.

Crossover Icky Shuffle

1. Start in the ready position at the near end of the ladder with both feet on the left side of the ladder.

2. Step across your body with your left foot and place it in the first square. Quickly step with your right foot across the ladder to the outside of the first square. Immediately follow with your left foot, stepping outside the first square. Your head and shoulders stay square and you face forward as your hips turn and rotate before steps 2 and 3 outside the ladder.

3. Once the left foot touches, quickly step across your body with your right foot and place it in the second square. Once the right foot touches, immediately step the left foot and right foot outside the second square, following the same sequence.

4. Continue this "in, out, out" sequence the length of the ladder.

HURDLE DRILLS

Three-Way Hurdle

Setup: Set 10 minihurdles (6 to 10 inches high, or 15 to 25 cm) 3 feet (about 1 m) apart from each other as shown in the illustration: 2 hurdles forward, 2 to the right, 2 forward, 2 to the left, 2 forward. The distance between a hurdle and the change of direction is also 3 feet.

1. Start in the ready position, facing the first hurdle.

2. Run forward over the first 2 hurdles (figure 7.4).

3. Shuffle to the right over the next 2 hurdles.

4. Run forward over the next 2 hurdles.

5. Shuffle to the left over the next 2 hurdles.

6. Run forward over the last 2 hurdles.

Advanced version: Go down and back.

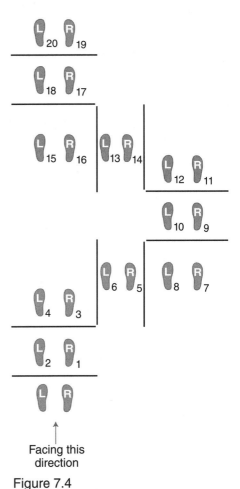

Figure 7.4

Diagonal Crossover Hurdle

Setup: Set 12 minihurdles (6 to 10 inches high, or 15 to 25 cm) 3 feet (about 1 m) apart from each other as shown in the illustration: 2 hurdles forward, 2 at a 45-degree angle to the right, 2 at a 45-degree angle to the left, 2 at a 45-degree angle to the right, 2 at a 45-degree angle to the left, and 2 forward. Hurdles may be adjusted closer together or farther apart as needed.

1. Start in the ready position facing the first hurdle.
2. Run over the first 2 hurdles (figure 7.5).
3. Do a crossover run to the right, leading with your right shoulder over the next 2 hurdles.
4. Do a crossover run to the left, leading with your left shoulder over the next 2 hurdles.
5. Do a crossover run to the right, leading with your right shoulder over the next 2 hurdles.
6. Do a crossover run to the left, leading with your left shoulder over the next 2 hurdles, and then run forward over the last 2 hurdles.
7. When leading with your right shoulder, cross your left foot over the midline of your body. When leading with your left shoulder, cross your right foot over the midline.

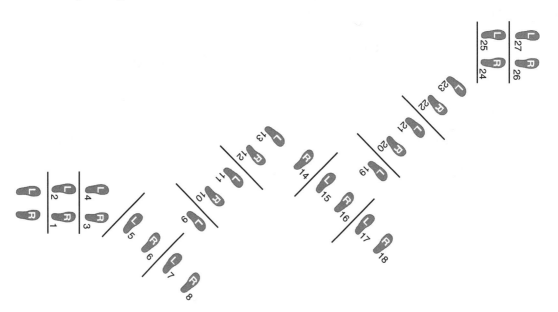

Figure 7.5

SNAKE DRILLS

Distances between cones for Snake Drills can range from 4 feet and greater for the Snake Run to 6 feet and greater for the Shuffle, Shuffle, Sprint and the Sprint, Backpedal, Shuffle, Shuffle.

Snake Run

Setup: Set 8 cones in a consistent staggered pattern.

1. Start in the ready position at the first cone, facing the second cone.
2. Sprint around the outside of each cone quickly and under control.

Shuffle, Shuffle, Sprint

Setup: Set 7 cones in a consistent staggered pattern.

1. Start in the ready position at the first cone with your right side facing the second cone.
2. Shuffle to your right around the second cone, turn slightly, and shuffle to your left around the third cone.
3. Sprint around the fourth cone.
4. Repeat this "shuffle, shuffle, sprint" pattern, starting with a shuffle to your left.

Sprint, Backpedal, Shuffle, Shuffle

Setup: Set 9 cones in a consistent staggered pattern.

1. Start in the ready position at the first cone, facing the second cone.
2. Sprint around the second cone.
3. Backpedal around the third cone.
4. Shuffle left around the fourth cone.
5. Shuffle right around the fifth cone.
6. Repeat this "sprint, backpedal, shuffle, shuffle" pattern, starting with a sprint.

LANE DRILLS

Lane Shuffle, Sprint, Backpedal

1. Start in the ready position at the right corner of the baseline and lane, facing the court.
2. Shuffle to your left across the lane. Touch the line with your left foot, change directions, and shuffle back to the start.
3. Immediately sprint up the free-throw lane line to the free-throw line. Shuffle to your left across the lane and back.
4. Quickly backpedal to the starting position.

Caution: Be aware of the baseline wall during the backpedal finish.

Lane Agility

This drill is the same as the Lane Agility Test in chapter 1 (page 6).

Setup: Set a cone in each of the 4 corners of the free-throw lane.

1. Start in the ready position outside the left-hand corner of the free-throw line extended, facing the baseline.
2. Sprint to the baseline past the cone. Defensive shuffle to the right past the cone. Backpedal to the free-throw line past the cone, and defensive shuffle to the left to the starting edge of the free-throw lane.
3. Immediately change directions and defensive shuffle to the right past the cone, sprint to the baseline past the cone, defensive shuffle left past the cone, and backpedal through the starting line.

Four Corners

1. Start in the ready position at the center of the lane facing the free-throw line.
2. Sprint to corner 1 and backpedal back to the start (figure 7.6).
3. Shuffle to the right to corner 2 and shuffle to the left back to the start.
4. Backpedal to corner 3 and sprint back to the start.
5. Shuffle to the left to corner 4 and shuffle to the right back to the start.

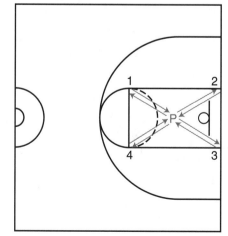

Figure 7.6

Jump, Shuffle, Jump

1. Start in the ready position in front of and below the right edge of the backboard, facing the baseline.
2. Jump up as high as possible with both hands above your head. Touch the backboard if you are able.
3. Land on both feet and immediately shuffle left. Jump as high as possible in front of the left edge of the backboard.
4. Shuffle back to the right edge of the backboard and jump as high as possible.
5. Continue this over-and-back pattern for 3 to 5 repetitions.

EXTENDED-LANE DRILLS

Acceleration, Deceleration, Backpedal, Jump, and Shuffle

Setup: Set 4 cones 3 feet apart along the free-throw line extended, starting 3 feet from the left sideline. Set cones at 3 feet, 6 feet, 9 feet, and 12 feet from the sideline (slightly less than 1, 2, 3, and 4 m).

1. Start in the ready position behind the left corner of the baseline and sideline, facing the court.
2. Sprint to the first cone and backpedal to the baseline (figure 7.7).
3. Sprint to the second cone and backpedal to the baseline.
4. Sprint to the third cone and backpedal to the baseline.
5. Sprint to the fourth cone and backpedal to the baseline and the edge of the lane.
6. Immediately jump as high as possible and then shuffle across the lane on the baseline and back.

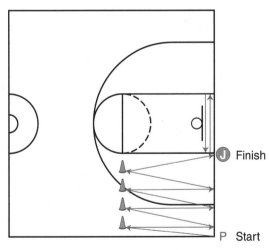

Figure 7.7

Caution: Do not step on the cones.

Advanced version: Repeat the drill all the way back to the starting position.

Four-Way Closeout

Setup: This drill is done along the free-throw lane (see figure 3.13, page 57).

1. Start in the ready position at the baseline along the left side of the lane, facing the court.
2. Sprint up the lane to the free-throw line and stop quickly in a defensive stance.
3. Shuffle left at a 45-degree angle for 2 shuffles and right for 2 shuffles, then backpedal to the start.
4. Repeat this sequence on the right side of the lane.

 ## Five-Spot Closeout

Setup: Spread out 5 cones evenly around the three-point arc.

1. Start in the ready position under the basket, facing the court.
2. Sprint to the first cone, jump stop, and backpedal to the start (figure 7.8).
3. Repeat the sequence to the second, third, fourth, and fifth cones.

Advanced version: A coach or teammate stands at the first cone with a basketball. Sprint to the coach and react to the coach. If the coach pump fakes, react to block the shot. If the coach moves to the right or left, defensive shuffle a step or two to cut off the coach. Immediately backpedal to the start as the coach moves to the second cone. Repeat the sequence to the second, third, fourth, and fifth cones.

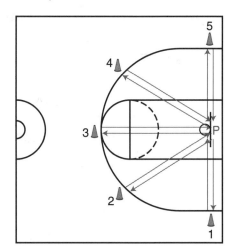

Figure 7.8

FULL-COURT DRILLS

Circle Run

1. Start in the ready position on the baseline at the end of the right lane, facing the court.
2. Run up the right lane and run counterclockwise around the first jump circle (figure 7.9).
3. Continue to the left of the half-court jump circle and run clockwise around the circle.
4. Continue to the right of the far jump circle and run counterclockwise around it. Finish at the baseline.
5. Return from the left lane so the pattern on the way back is opposite.

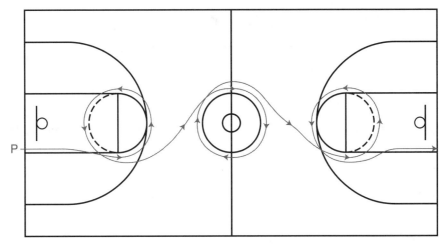

Figure 7.9

Backpedal, Hip Rotation, Sprint

Setup: Set 3 cones in a staggered pattern on the free-throw lane lines extended between the free-throw lines (see figure 3.12, page 56).

1. Start in the ready position behind the baseline in the middle of the free-throw lane, facing away from the court.
2. Backpedal to the free-throw line, turn with good hip rotation, and sprint around the 3 cones to the far free-throw line.
3. Turn with good hip rotation and backpedal to the baseline.

Caution: Be aware of the baseline wall during the backpedal finish.

Advanced version: Vary the distances between the cones.

High-Speed Sprint Agility

Setup: Set 3 cones in a staggered pattern, 1 on the right sideline at half court and 2 on the center of each half court.

1. Start in the ready position at the right corner of the baseline and sideline, facing the court.
2. Sprint around the 3 cones as fast as possible and finish at the far-right baseline corner.

Advanced version: Set the cones closer together. Set the cones at the sideline and near the free-throw lane line or set the cones on the free-throw lane lines extended.

Chapter 8

Complete Conditioning Schedule

The off-season is the most important time of the year to make your best gains. You can become stronger, faster, more powerful, and quicker. Each component in the 12-Week Off-Season Program will help you to become a better basketball player. To become your best, you must consistently train all the components of the 12-Week Off-Season Program. The strength training workout cards at the end of the chapter will help you record and track your programs.

COMPONENTS

The warm-up, stretching, and cool-down will help to reduce injuries and improve performance. Strength training will increase your performance by improving strength, speed, power, quickness, and flexibility. Your improved conditioning will help you become a better basketball player, allowing you to play at higher intensities for longer periods of time and giving your team a better chance of winning. Plyometrics will improve your explosive power so you will jump higher and run faster. Agility training will improve your quickness and your ability to change directions.

CALENDAR

The calendar on the following pages shows you how the 12-Week Complete Conditioning Program fits together. When you begin the program, the exercises should be low intensity and high volume. The low-intensity, high-volume phase is followed by a higher-intensity, lower-volume phase, with a peaking phase at the end of the program. The 12-week calendar is for you to use as a daily check to monitor your complete conditioning program.

Some highly motivated athletes may want to do more than what we recommend on a daily basis. That can lead to overtraining, a decrease in performance, and possible injuries. For best results, follow the program as outlined.

COMPLETE CONDITIONING OPTIONS AND TRANSITIONS

Choose from the following program options and transitions for the 12-Week Complete Conditioning Program.

- You may switch your Monday–Thursday workout days with your Tuesday–Friday workout days. Possible reasons to switch days may include facility scheduling (track, basketball court, weight room), your and your partner's schedule, or if you have an upper-body strength priority.

- You may do conditioning, plyometrics, and agility before strength training if you have a priority in any of these areas.

- The Four-Day Complete Conditioning Program allows you to make up a missed workout the next day and still fit all your training days in during the week.

- Be aware of the transitions from strides to track sprints (starting week 5) and track sprints to court sprints (starting week 7).

- Be aware of the transitions in strength training sets and repetitions. Upper-body transitions occur during weeks 4, 6, 10, and 11 of the 12-Week Off-Season Cycle. Lower-body transitions occur during weeks 3, 5, 9, and 11 of the 12-Week Off-Season Cycle.

- The speed drills are not listed on the 12-week calendar. The speed drills can be performed on Wednesdays and Saturdays. The advanced speed drills should not be performed before week 7.

Dirk Nowitzki of the Dallas Mavericks shoots a three over Andrera Bargnani of the Toronto Raptors.

© Warren Toda/epa/Corbis

SAMPLE OFF-SEASON DAILY WORKOUTS

The off-season sample workouts involve four main training days per week. The Monday and Thursday workouts include warm-up, stretch, lower-body strength training, conditioning, and cool-down. The Tuesday and Friday workouts include warm-up, stretch, upper-body strength training, plyometrics, agility, and cool-down (table 8.1). Remember the off-season is the time for you to make the best gains. The strength training workouts consist of a Four-Day Split Program. The two different workouts are explained in detail in the following pages. The conditioning workouts are on Mondays and Thursdays. Refer to the 12-Week Off-Season Conditioning Program in chapter 3, Conditioning (page 51). The plyometric and agility training is done on Tuesdays and Fridays. Refer to the five variables in the section titled Program Development in chapter 5, Power (page 130). Also refer to the off-season information in the Yearly Training Schedule section in chapter 7, Agility (page 173).

Table 8.1 Off-Season Workouts: Week 1

Monday	Tuesday	Wednesday	Thursday	Friday
Warm-up	Warm-up	Off	Warm-up	Warm-up
Stretch	Stretch		Stretch	Stretch
Weight train: lower body	Weight train: upper body		Weight train: lower body	Weight train: upper body
Conditioning strides	Plyometrics Agility		Conditioning strides	Plyometrics Agility
Cool-down	Cool-down		Cool-down	Cool-down

Monday's Workout

Warm-Up This warm-up and stretching program is from chapter 2, Warm-Up and Flexibility. Do various movements up and down the court before stretching: High Knee Run, Butt Kick, High Knee Skip, Carioca, Lateral Shuffle, Walking Lunge, and Backward Run. After the movements up and down the court, do the Side-to-Side Kick and Front-and-Back Kick.

Stretching Follow the Basic Stretch from chapter 2, Warm-Up and Flexibility.

Upper-Body Stretches: Arm Circle, Pec Stretch, Lat Stretch, External and Internal Shoulder Rotation, Lateral Trunk Stretch

Lower-Body Stretches: Knees to Chest, Leg Crossover, Glute Stretch, Lower-Back Stretch, Bent-Knee Hamstring Stretch, Straight-Leg Hamstring Stretch, Seated Groin Stretch, Quad Stretch, Straight-Leg Calf Stretch, and Bent-Knee Calf Stretch

Lower-Body Strength Training The following is an example of an Off-Season Lower-Body Strength Training Program with options. Refer to the Four-Day Split Program in chapter 4, Strength, in the Off-Season Program section (page 119) before you choose your daily workout.

Hang Clean or Hang Pull

Squat or Leg Press

Hamstring Curl

Lunge, Step-Up, or Leg Extension

Straight-Leg Deadlift or Back Extension

Side Lunge or Abduction, Adduction

Standing Calf Raise

Core—Lower Back

Core—Abs

Conditioning Table 8.2 is the Monday on-court conditioning workout for week 10 of the 12-Week Conditioning Program.

Cool-Down Like a good warm-up, a postworkout cool-down is important. It enhances the recovery of the muscles and helps the body return to its resting state. A good cool-down includes light exercise and stretching of the major muscle groups—the lower back, glutes, hamstrings, quads, and groin.

Table 8.2 On-Court Conditioning Workout: Week 10—Day 1

Week	Day	Workout	Rest time
10	Day 1	Full-Court Sprint Dribble × 1	1 min.
		Full-Court Zigzag Sprint Dribble × 1	1 min.
		Sideline Sprint Layup × 2	1 min.
		X Drill × 2	2 min.
		Deep 6s × 2	1 min.

Tuesday's Workout

Warm-Up This warm-up and stretching program is from chapter 2, Warm-Up and Flexibility. Do various movements up and down the court before stretching: High Knee Run, Butt Kick, High Knee Skip, Carioca, Lateral Shuffle, Walking Lunge, and Backward Run. After the movements up and down the court, do the Side-to-Side Kick and Front-and-Back Kick.

Stretching   Follow the Full Stretch from chapter 2, Warm-Up and Flexibility.

Neck Stretches: Neck Semicircle, Chin to Chest, Look-Up, Ear to Shoulder, Neck Rotation

Upper-Body Stretches: Arm Circle, Pec Stretch, Lat Stretch, External and Internal Shoulder Rotation, Lateral Trunk Stretch

Lower-Body Stretches: Knees to Chest, Leg Crossover, Glute Stretch, Lower-Back Stretch, Bent-Knee Hamstring Stretch, Straight-Leg Hamstring Stretch, Seated Groin Stretch, Quad Stretch, Straight-Leg Calf Stretch, and Bent-Knee Calf Stretch

Upper-Body Strength Training   The following is an example of an Off-Season Upper-Body Strength Training Program with options. Refer to the Four-Day Split Program in chapter 4, Strength, in the Off-Season Program section (page 119) before you choose your daily workout.

Bench Press

Pull-Up or Lat Pulldown

Incline Bench Press

Seated Lat Row or Dumbbell Lat Row

Shoulder Press or Push Press

Upright Row or Lateral Raise

Triceps Press-Down or Bar Dip

Biceps Curl

Core—Abs

Plyometric Training   There are 33 plyometric exercises from beginning to advanced in 5 categories in chapter 5, Power. Pick 6 to 12 plyometric exercises per workout, depending on your exercise level. Here is a sample plyometric workout with 2 exercises from each category.

Double-Leg Hop

Double-Leg Box Circuit

Single-Leg Forward Barrier Jump

Single-Leg Lateral Barrier Jump

Quick-Step Box Touch

Lateral Box Shuffle

Medicine Ball Chest Pass

Medicine Ball Side Pass

Double-Leg Power Dunk or Layup

Single-Leg Power Dunk or Layup

Make sure you count the total number of foot contacts in each workout and stay within your category (beginning, intermediate, or advanced).

Agility Training   There are 20 agility drills in chapter 7, Agility. Pick 6 to 8 types of agility drills per workout. Here are sample drills used in an agility workout.

Hurdle Drills
Three-Way Hurdle Drill

Diagonal Crossover Hurdle Drill

Snake Drills
Snake Run

Shuffle, Shuffle, Sprint

Lane Drills
Lane Agility

Four-Way Closeout

Cool-Down   Like a good warm-up, a postworkout cool-down is important. It enhances the recovery of the muscles and helps the body return to its resting state. A good cool-down includes light exercise and stretching of the major muscle groups—the lower back, glutes, hamstrings, quads, and groin.

SAMPLE IN-SEASON DAILY WORKOUTS

The in-season sample workouts include warm-up, stretch, practice, extra conditioning if needed, strength training, and cool-down. Many plyometric and agility movements are performed during a full basketball practice. Therefore, in-season plyometric and agility drills should be limited if used at all. Please refer to the note on in-season volume in the section titled Program Development in chapter 5, Power (page 130). Also refer to the in-season information in the yearly training schedule in chapter 7, Agility (page 173). The daily sample workouts for the in-season have strength training after practice, but you may also do strength training before practice. During the in-season, the majority of your conditioning comes from practices and games. If your practices include intense all-out drills, running the court hard, and good defensive work for at least 1 hour, you probably don't need extra conditioning. If you do need extra conditioning, you may choose from the on-court conditioning drills in chapter 3, Conditioning.

Warm-up

Stretch

Practice

Extra conditioning

Strength training

Cool-down

Warm-Up This warm-up and stretching program is from chapter 2, Warm-Up and Flexibility. Do various movements up and down the court before stretching: High Knee Run, Butt Kick, High Knee Skip, Carioca, Lateral Shuffle, Walking Lunge, and Backward Run. After the movements up and down the court, do the Side-to-Side Kick and Front-and-Back Kick.

Stretching Follow the Full Stretch from chapter 2, Warm-Up and Flexibility.

Neck Stretches: Neck Semicircle, Chin to Chest, Look-Up, Ear to Shoulder, Neck Rotation

Upper-Body Stretches: Arm Circle, Pec Stretch, Lat Stretch, External and Internal Shoulder Rotation, Lateral Trunk Stretch

Lower-Body Stretches: Knees to Chest, Leg Crossover, Glute Stretch, Lower-Back Stretch, Bent-Knee Hamstring Stretch, Straight-Leg Hamstring Stretch, Seated Groin Stretch, Quad Stretch, Straight-Leg Calf Stretch, and Bent-Knee Calf Stretch

Basketball Practice

Extra Conditioning if needed If you do need extra conditioning, you may choose from the on-court conditioning drills in chapter 3, Conditioning.

Strength Training Before you choose your daily workout, refer to the in-season program options in chapter 4, Strength, to see how those variables apply to you.

Cool-Down Like a good warm-up, a postworkout cool-down is important. It enhances the recovery of the muscles and helps the body return to its resting state. A good cool-down includes light exercise and stretching of the major muscle groups—the lower back, glutes, hamstrings, quads, and groin.

STRENGTH TRAINING WORKOUT CARDS

The Four-Day Split workout cards match the 12-Week Off-Season Cycles (tables 4.5 and 4.6, pages 125 and 126). Make 5 to 10 copies of the workout cards and always keep blank master copies for future needs. The numbers on the cards represent the exercises that should be done together as a superset, which was explained in chapter 4, Strength, under the Four-Day Split Program. The superset numbered exercise combinations are listed on the Four-Day Split, the Three-Day Total-Body, and the Total-Body In-Season workout cards. The Total-Body Circuit and the Combo workouts should be done in the order listed.

When supersetting, do the first set of each exercise before progressing to the second set of each exercise. Continue this alternating pattern for the prescribed sets and repetitions for each of the exercises supersetted throughout the program.

Exercises	Wt. x reps
1. Bench press (bar, dumbbell, or machine)	100 x 15
	135 x 10
	155 x 8
	185 x 6

Use the workout cards to keep track of your program. At the top of each card, write your name, and in each daily column record your body weight and the date. In the small boxes next to each exercise, list your sets and repetitions. List the weight first and then your repetitions. The top box is the first set, the second box is the second set, and so on. Here is an example of a four-set Bench Press workout:

Each card has exercise options for most numbered exercises to fit your specific needs: equipment available, favorite exercises, physical limitations, and so on. If you follow the numbers and prescribed repetitions, you will have a functional program that increases performance and reduces the chances of injury.

Four-Day Split Lower-Body Workout Card

Name

	Wt. × reps	Wt. × reps	Wt. × reps	Wt. × reps	Wt. × reps	Wt. × reps
Body weight						
Date						
Exercises						
1. Hang Clean or Hang Pull						
2. Squat or Leg Press						
2. Hamstring Curl (lying, single-leg, seated, or standing)						
3. Lunge, Step-Up, or Leg Extension						
3. Straight-Leg Deadlift or Back Extension						
4. Side Lunge or Abduction, Adduction (12-15)						
4. Standing Calf Raise (15-25)						
5. Core—lower back (pick 2: trunk extension, hip extension, total core)						
5. Core—abs (pick 3: trunk flexion, hip flexion, rotary)						

From National Basketball Conditioning Coaches Association, 2007, *Complete Conditioning for Basketball* (Champaign, IL: Human Kinetics).

Four-Day Split Upper-Body Workout Card

Name

Exercises	Wt. × reps	Wt. × reps	Wt. × reps	Wt. × reps	Wt. × reps	Wt. × reps
Body weight						
Date						
1. Bench Press (bar, dumbbell, or machine)						
1. Pull-Up or Lat Pulldown (front or behind)						
2. Incline Bench Press (bar, dumbell, or machine)						
2. Seated Lat Row or Dumbbell Lat Row						
3. Shoulder Press (bar or dumbbell, seated or standing) (first 6 weeks) 3. Push Press (second 6 weeks)						
3. Upright Row or Dumbbell Lateral Raise						
4. Bar Dip or Triceps Press-Down						
4. Biceps Curl (bar or dumbbell)						
5. Core—abs (pick 4: trunk flexion, hip flexion, rotary)						

From National Basketball Conditioning Coaches Association, 2007, *Complete Conditioning for Basketball* (Champaign, IL: Human Kinetics).

Three-Day Total Body Workout Card, Monday and Friday

Name

Exercises	Wt. × reps	Wt. × reps	Wt. × reps	Wt. × reps	Wt. × reps	Wt. × reps
Body weight						
Date						
1. Hang Clean						
2. Squat or Leg Press						
2. Hamstring Curl (lying, single-leg, seated, or standing)						
3. Step-Up or Leg Extension						
3. Straight-Leg Deadlift						
4. Side Lunge or Abduction, Adduction						
4. Standing Calf Raise						
5. Bench Press						
5. Lat Pulldown						
6. Push Press						
7. Triceps Press-Down						
7. Dumbbell Biceps Curl						
8. Core—abs						
8. Core—lower back						

From National Basketball Conditioning Coaches Association, 2007, *Complete Conditioning for Basketball* (Champaign, IL: Human Kinetics).

Three-Day Total Body Workout Card, Wednesday

Name

Exercises	Wt. × reps	Wt. × reps	Wt. × reps	Wt. × reps	Wt. × reps	Wt. × reps
Body weight						
Date						
1. Dumbbell Bench Press						
1. Pull-Up						
2. Dummbbell Incline Bench Press						
2. Dumbbell Lat Row or Seated Lat Row						
3. Dumbbell Lateral Raise						
3. Bar Dip						
3. Bar Biceps Curl						
4. Hang Pull						
5. Lunge						
5. Hamstring Curl						
6. Standing Calf Raise						
6. Back Extension						
7. Core—abs						
7. Core—lower back						

From National Basketball Conditioning Coaches Association, 2007, *Complete Conditioning for Basketball* (Champaign, IL: Human Kinetics).

In-Season Total-Body Workout Card

Name

Exercises	Body weight					
	Date					
	Wt. × reps	Wt. × reps	Wt. × reps	Wt. × reps	Wt. × reps	Wt. × reps
Bench Press or Incline Press (bar, dumbbell, or machine)						
Pull-Up, Lat Pulldown, or Lat Row						
Upright Row (bar or dumbbell) or Lateral Shoulder Raise (machine or dumbbell)						
Biceps Curl (bar or dumbbell)						
Triceps Extension or Triceps Press						
Core—abs (pick 4: trunk flexion, hip flexion, rotary)						
Hang Pull or Hang Clean						
Squat, Leg Press, Lunge, Step-Up, or Leg Extension						
Hamstring Curl (lying, single-leg, seated, or standing)						
Abduction, Adduction (machine, single-leg pulley, or tubing)						
Straight-Leg Deadlift or Back Extension						

From National Basketball Conditioning Coaches Association, 2007, *Complete Conditioning for Basketball* (Champaign, IL: Human Kinetics).

197

In-Season Total-Body Circuit Workout Card

Name

	Wt. × reps	Wt. × reps	Wt. × reps	Wt. × reps	Wt. × reps	Wt. × reps
Body weight						
Date						
Exercises						
Leg Press						
Bench Press						
Lat Pull-Down						
Leg Curl						
Seated Dumbbell Shoulder Press						
Abs—Crunch						
Step-Up						
Triceps Press-Down or Bar Dip						
Dumbbell Biceps Curl						
Back Extensions						
Standing Calf Raise						
Abs—Leg Raise						

From National Basketball Conditioning Coaches Association, 2007, *Complete Conditioning for Basketball* (Champaign, IL: Human Kinetics).

Index

Note: The italicized *f* and *t* following page numbers refers to figures or tables that illustrate the topic.

About the NBCCA

The National Basketball Conditioning Coaches Association (NBCCA) is a select group of strength and conditioning coaches from teams in the National Basketball Association. The NBCCA was founded in 1992 by Bill Foran of the Miami Heat, Robin Pound (formerly of the Phoenix Suns and the WNBA's Phoenix Mercury), and Bob King of the Dallas Mavericks. The association's mission is to develop and promote strength and conditioning throughout basketball, particularly at the professional level. The NBCCA provides an opportunity for strength and conditioning coaches in the league to network, keep updated on new information, work together on various projects, and promote strength and conditioning for basketball at all levels.

About the Project Coordinators

Bill Foran is project coordinator for the book and is cofounder of the National Basketball Conditioning Coaches Association. He has been the strength and conditioning coach for the Miami Heat since 1989. Before working for the Heat, Foran was the head strength and conditioning coach at Washington State University (1981 to 1985) and the University of Miami (1985 to 1989). Foran earned a bachelor's degree in health education and physical education from Central Michigan University and a master's degree in exercise physiology from Michigan State University.

Courtesy of the Miami Heat

Robin Pound is associate coordinator for the book and is cofounder of the National Basketball Conditioning Coaches Association. He was the strength and conditioning coach for the Phoenix Suns from 1991 to 2003 and the WNBA's Phoenix Mercury from 1997 to 2003. Pound was an assistant strength and conditioning coach for the University of Oregon from 1979 to 1985 and the head strength and conditioning coach at the University of California at Berkeley from 1985 to 1991. Pound earned a bachelor's degree in physical education and a teaching degree from the University of Oregon, where he also earned a master's degree in exercise physiology and anatomy.

Courtesy of the Phoenix Suns

About the Contributors

Al Biancani retired in 2005 after 18 years as the strength and conditioning coach of the Sacramento Kings. He was also strength and conditioning coach of the Sacramento Monarchs of the WNBA. Coach Biancani contributed to chapter 5, Power.

Mike Brungardt has been strength and conditioning coach for the San Antonio Spurs since 1994. Coach Brungardt contributed to chapter 4, Strength.

Dwight Daub has been strength and conditioning coach for the Seattle Sonics since 1997. Coach Daub contributed to chapter 1, Tests and Evaluation.

Bill Dean served as the strength and conditioning coach for the Indiana Pacers from 1998 to 2005. Coach Dean contributed to chapter 5, Power.

Robert Hackett has been the strength and conditioning coach for the Dallas Mavericks since 2002. Previously he spent 7 seasons as strength and conditioning coach with the Memphis Grizzlies. Coach Hackett contributed to chapter 6, Speed, and to chapter 7, Agility.

Steve Hess has been the strength and conditioning coach for the Denver Nuggets since 1996. Coach Hess contributed information on core training to chapter 4, Strength.

Pete Radulovic has been the strength and conditioning coach for the Atlanta Hawks since 1997. Coach Radulovic contributed to chapter 1, Tests and Evaluation.

Mick Smith was the strength and conditioning coach for the Orlando Magic from 1996 to 2006. Previously he spent 4 years as the strength and conditioning coach for the Portland Trail Blazers. Coach Smith contributed to chapter 3, Conditioning.

Tim Wilson has been the strength and conditioning coach of the Milwaukee Bucks since 1998. Coach Wilson contributed information on core training to chapter 4, Strength.

You'll find other outstanding basketball resources at

http://basketball.humankinetics.com

In the U.S. call 1-800-747-4457

Australia (08) 8372 0999 • Canada 1-800-465-7301
Europe +44 (0) 113 255 5665 • New Zealand 0064 9 448 1207